The Modern Mindset

The Modern Mindset

Understanding Personality, Emotions, and Everyday Decisions

A Practical Workbook for Self-Awareness and Growth

John Snape

THRIVE
WORKBOOKS

The Modern Mindset: Understanding Personality, Emotions, and Everyday Decisions

© 2026 Thrive Workbooks

All rights reserved. No part of this publication may be reproduced, distributed, or transmitted in any form or by any means — electronic, mechanical, photocopying, recording, or otherwise — without prior written permission of the publisher, except in the case of brief quotations used in reviews or critical articles.

For information, contact:
Thrive Workbooks
Escondido, California, United States
https://thriveworkbooks.com/

ISBN: 978-1-948593-99-1

Disclaimer

This workbook is intended for informational and educational purposes only. It is not a substitute for professional psychological, psychiatric, medical, or counseling advice, diagnosis, or treatment. Readers are encouraged to consult a qualified health-care or mental-health professional for any questions or concerns regarding their own emotional or psychological condition.

The author and publisher make no representations or warranties regarding the accuracy, completeness, or applicability of the information contained herein. Neither shall be held liable for any loss, injury, or damages arising from the use of this material or from reliance on information contained in this book.

Use of this workbook constitutes acceptance of these terms and acknowledgment that self-reflection activities are undertaken at the reader's discretion and risk.

This workbook is based on the personality typology originally described by Carl Jung and further developed by Katharine Cook Briggs and Isabel Briggs Myers. The Myers–Briggs Type Indicator® and MBTI® are registered trademarks of The Myers & Briggs Foundation, which has neither reviewed nor endorsed this material.

The Myers–Briggs Type Indicator®, Myers–Briggs®, MBTI®, and the MBTI® logo are trademarks or registered trademarks of The Myers & Briggs Foundation, Inc., and The Myers & Briggs Company. This publication is an independent work and has not been reviewed or endorsed by either organization.

Printed in the United States of America

Table of Contents

Foreword
- Part I: Personality and Type 3
- Part II: Personality and Mental Health 3
- Part III: Personality in Context 4
- Appendices: Practical Frameworks for Growth 4
- What You'll Gain 4
- Notes on Attribution 5

Preface
- Why This Book Exists 6
- What This Book Is and Isn't 6
- Why the Appendices Exist 7
- What You Will Gain 7
- Project Purpose 7

How to Use This Workbook
- The Workbook Format 9
- Why the MBTI Comes First 9
- How to Read the Book 10
- Using the Exercises 10
- The Spirit of the Work 10

The Architecture of Personality
- A Brief History of Understanding the Mind 11
- From Temperament to Type 11
- Psychology Becomes a Science 11
- From Typology to Measurement 12
- The Broader History of Psychiatry and Psychology 13
- Why This History Matters 13
- Looking Ahead 13

Part I: Understanding the Myers–Briggs Type Indicator (MBTI)
- The Origin of the System 14
- Jung's Insight: The Machinery of the Mind 14
- From Theory to Practical Application 15
- A Tool for Understanding, Not Judgment 15
- The Four Core Dichotomies 15
  - 1. Extraversion (E) / Introversion (I) 15

2. Sensing (S) / Intuition (N) 16
3. Thinking (T) / Feeling (F) 16
4. Judging (J) / Perceiving (P) 17
Who Uses the MBTI and Why 17
Other Major Personality Frameworks 17
Alternate Personality Frameworks Explained 18
    1. Temperament Theory (Keirsey) 18
    2. The Big Five Personality Model (OCEAN) 18
    3. The Enneagram of Personality 19
    4. Socionics 19
Perspective 20
Interpreting MBTI: Your Type 20
The Four-Letter Code 20
Cognitive Functions: The Engine Beneath the Surface 21
Type Dynamics 22
The Shadow Functions 22
How to Read Type Descriptions 22
Purpose of Typology 23
A Word of Caution: Understanding vs. Labeling 23
Discovering Your Type 24
Self-Assessment: Discovering Your Preferences 25
    1. Extraversion (E) vs. Introversion (I) 25
    2. Sensing (S) vs. Intuition (N) 25
    3. Thinking (T) vs. Feeling (F) 25
    4. Judging (J) vs. Perceiving (P) 26
Interpreting Your Type 26
    Compatibility Notes 26
ISTJ – The Inspector 27
    Core Traits 27
    Cognitive Overview 27
    Temperament as a Child 27
    Temperament as an Adult 28
    Best Learning Style 28
    Workplace Habits 28
    Friendships 28
    Love Life 29
    Money Management 29
    Best Parts of the Type 29
    Worst Parts of the Type 29
    Growth and Development 30

- ISTJ Compatibility ... 30
- **ISFJ – The Protector** ... 31
  - Core Traits ... 31
  - Cognitive Overview ... 31
  - Temperament as a Child ... 31
  - Temperament as an Adult ... 31
  - Best Learning Style ... 32
  - Workplace Habits ... 32
  - Friendships ... 32
  - Love Life ... 32
  - Money Management ... 33
  - Best Parts of the Type ... 33
  - Worst Parts of the Type ... 33
  - Growth and Development ... 33
  - ISFJ Compatibility ... 34
- **INFJ – The Counselor** ... 35
  - Core Traits ... 35
  - Cognitive Overview ... 35
  - Temperament as a Child ... 35
  - Temperament as an Adult ... 36
  - Best Learning Style ... 36
  - Workplace Habits ... 36
  - Friendships ... 36
  - Love Life ... 37
  - Money Management ... 37
  - Best Parts of the Type ... 37
  - Worst Parts of the Type ... 37
  - Growth and Development ... 37
  - INFJ Compatibility ... 38
- **INTJ – The Mastermind** ... 39
  - Core Traits ... 39
  - Cognitive Overview ... 39
  - Temperament as a Child ... 39
  - Temperament as an Adult ... 40
  - Best Learning Style ... 40
  - Workplace Habits ... 40
  - Friendships ... 40
  - Love Life ... 41
  - Money Management ... 41
  - Best Parts of the Type ... 41

- Worst Parts of the Type 41
- Growth and Development 41
- INTJ Compatibility 42

ISTP – The Crafter 43
- Core Traits 43
- Cognitive Overview 43
- Temperament as a Child 43
- Temperament as an Adult 44
- Best Learning Style 44
- Workplace Habits 44
- Friendships 44
- Love Life 44
- Money Management 45
- Best Parts of the Type 45
- Worst Parts of the Type 45
- Growth and Development 45
- ISTP Compatibility 46

ISFP – The Composer 47
- Core Traits 47
- Cognitive Overview 47
- Temperament as a Child 47
- Temperament as an Adult 48
- Best Learning Style 48
- Workplace Habits 48
- Friendships 48
- Love Life 49
- Money Management 49
- Best Parts of the Type 49
- Worst Parts of the Type 49
- Growth and Development 50
- ISFP Compatibility 50

INFP – The Healer 51
- Core Traits 51
- Cognitive Overview 51
- Temperament as a Child 51
- Temperament as an Adult 51
- Best Learning Style 52
- Workplace Habits 52
- Friendships 52
- Love Life 53

- Money Management 53
- Best Parts of the Type 53
- Worst Parts of the Type 53
- Growth and Development 54
- INFP Compatibility 54

INTP – The Architect 55
- Core Traits 55
- Cognitive Overview 55
- Temperament as a Child 55
- Temperament as an Adult 55
- Best Learning Style 56
- Workplace Habits 56
- Friendships 56
- Love Life 56
- Money Management 57
- Best Parts of the Type 57
- Worst Parts of the Type 57
- Growth and Development 57
- INTP Compatibility 58

ESTP – The Dynamo 59
- Core Traits 59
- Cognitive Overview 59
- Temperament as a Child 59
- Temperament as an Adult 60
- Best Learning Style 60
- Workplace Habits 60
- Friendships 60
- Love Life 61
- Money Management 61
- Best Parts of the Type 61
- Worst Parts of the Type 61
- Growth and Development 62
- ESTP Compatibility 62

ESFP – The Performer 63
- Core Traits 63
- Cognitive Overview 63
- Temperament as a Child 63
- Temperament as an Adult 64
- Best Learning Style 64
- Workplace Habits 64

  Friendships...64
  Love Life...65
  Money Management.......................................65
  Best Parts of the Type....................................65
  Worst Parts of the Type..................................65
  Growth and Development................................66
  ESFP Compatibility..66

ENFP – The Champion..67
  Core Traits...67
  Cognitive Overview..67
  Temperament as a Child..................................67
  Temperament as an Adult................................67
  Best Learning Style..68
  Workplace Habits..68
  Friendships...68
  Love Life...69
  Money Management.......................................69
  Best Parts of the Type....................................69
  Worst Parts of the Type..................................69
  Growth and Development................................70
  ENFP Compatibility..70

ENTP – The Visionary..71
  Core Traits...71
  Cognitive Overview..71
  Temperament as a Child..................................71
  Temperament as an Adult................................71
  Best Learning Style..72
  Workplace Habits..72
  Friendships...72
  Love Life...72
  Money Management.......................................73
  Best Parts of the Type....................................73
  Worst Parts of the Type..................................73
  Growth and Development................................73
  ENTP Compatibility..74

ESTJ – The Supervisor..75
  Core Traits...75
  Cognitive Overview..75
  Temperament as a Child..................................75
  Temperament as an Adult................................75

- Best Learning Style ... 76
- Workplace Habits ... 76
- Friendships ... 76
- Love Life ... 77
- Money Management ... 77
- Best Parts of the Type ... 77
- Worst Parts of the Type ... 77
- Growth and Development ... 78
- ESTJ Compatibility ... 78

ESFJ – The Provider ... 79
- Core Traits ... 79
- Cognitive Overview ... 79
- Temperament as a Child ... 79
- Temperament as an Adult ... 80
- Best Learning Style ... 80
- Workplace Habits ... 80
- Friendships ... 80
- Love Life ... 81
- Money Management ... 81
- Best Parts of the Type ... 81
- Worst Parts of the Type ... 81
- Growth and Development ... 82
- ESFJ Compatibility ... 82

ENFJ – The Teacher ... 83
- Core Traits ... 83
- Cognitive Overview ... 83
- Temperament as a Child ... 83
- Temperament as an Adult ... 84
- Best Learning Style ... 84
- Workplace Habits ... 84
- Friendships ... 84
- Love Life ... 85
- Money Management ... 85
- Best Parts of the Type ... 85
- Worst Parts of the Type ... 85
- Growth and Development ... 86
- ENFJ Compatibility ... 86
- Friendship ... 86

ENTJ – The Commander ... 87
- Core Traits ... 87

    Cognitive Overview 87
    Temperament as a Child 87
    Temperament as an Adult 88
    Best Learning Style 88
    Workplace Habits. 88
    Friendships 88
    Love Life. 89
    Money Management 89
    Best Parts of the Type 89
    Worst Parts of the Type 89
    Growth and Development 90
    ENTJ Compatibility. 90

Part II: Beyond Typology
    Chapter 1: Personality vs. Personality Disorder 91
        Introduction 91
        Healthy Personality 91
        Disordered Personality 91
        The Spectrum of Functioning 92
        Why the Distinction Matters. 92
        Reflection Exercise 92
        Summary. 93
    Chapter 2: Narcissism: The Spectrum, Not the Buzzword 94
        Introduction 94
        What Narcissism Actually Is. 94
        What Narcissism Is Not 94
        Recognizing the Pattern 94
        Healthy Self-Esteem vs. Narcissistic Defense 95
        Living or Working with Narcissistic Patterns 95
        Reflection Exercise 95
        Summary. 95
    Chapter 3: Psychopathy and Sociopathy: Coldness vs. Chaos .96
        Introduction 96
        What Psychopathy Is. 96
        What Sociopathy Is 96
        Key Differences 96
        Myths and Realities 97
        Dealing with Antisocial Patterns 97
        Reflection Exercise 97
        Summary. 97

Chapter 4: Borderline Personality Patterns: Intensity, Not Evil...........98
Introduction...........98
What Borderline Personality Disorder Is...........98
What It Is Not...........98
The Emotional Landscape...........98
Myths and Realities...........99
Living or Working with Borderline Patterns...........99
Reflection Exercise...........99
Summary...........99

Chapter 5: The Culture of Labels...........100
Introduction...........100
How Label Culture Took Hold...........100
The Real Cost of Mislabeling...........100
Why We Reach for Labels...........100
How to Talk About Behavior Responsibly...........101
A Better Vocabulary for Everyday Life...........101
Reflection Exercise...........101
Summary...........101

Part III: Personality and Mental Health
Chapter 1: Healthy Personality vs. Mental Disorder...........102
Introduction...........102
Flexibility vs. Rigidity...........102
Function, Not Fault...........102
How Personality and Mental Health Interact...........103
The Gray Zone: Traits vs. Disorders...........103
When to Seek Professional Help...........103
Reflection Exercise...........103
Summary...........104

Chapter 2: Mood and Emotional Disorders...........105
Introduction...........105
Depression: More Than Sadness...........105
Bipolar Disorder: The Cycle of Highs and Lows...........106
Anxiety Disorders: The Mind's False Alarms...........106
Reflection Exercise...........107
Summary...........107

Chapter 3: Neurodevelopmental Conditions...........108
Introduction...........108
Autism Spectrum Disorder (ASD)...........108
Attention-Deficit/Hyperactivity Disorder (ADHD)...........109

 Neurodiversity and Society...109
 Reflection Exercise 110
 Summary...110
Chapter 4: Obsessive-Compulsive Disorder and Related Patterns 111
 Introduction 111
 What OCD Is 111
 What OCD Is Not 111
 What Helps..111
 The Spectrum of Control 112
 Related Conditions 112
 Reflection Exercise 112
 Summary...113
Chapter 5: Related Disorders: Body Image, Hoarding, and Repetitive Behaviors ... 114
 Introduction 114
 Body Dysmorphic Disorder (BDD) 114
Eating Disorders: Anorexia and Bulimia.....................................114
 What They Are 114
 Anorexia Nervosa 115
 Bulimia Nervosa...115
 What Helps..115
 Hoarding Disorder...115
 Body-Focused Repetitive Behaviors (BFRBs) 116
 Common Threads 116
 Reflection Exercise 117
 Summary...117
Chapter 6: Psychotic and Thought Disorders.................................118
 Introduction 118
 What Psychosis Is 118
 Schizophrenia: The Prototype Disorder 118
 Schizoaffective Disorder 119
 Delusional Disorder...119
 Causes and Risk Factors 119
 Recovery and Management 120
 Reflection Exercise 120
 Summary...120
Chapter 7: Trauma and Stressor-Related Disorders...........................121
 Introduction 121
 Post-Traumatic Stress Disorder (PTSD) 121
 Complex PTSD (C-PTSD) 122
 Adjustment Disorders 122

- The Physiology of Trauma 123
- Reflection Exercise 123
- Summary 123

Chapter 8: Personality and the Brain: Biological and Cognitive Foundations 124
- Introduction 124
- The Brain's Architecture of Personality 124
- Neurochemistry and Temperament 124
- Genetics vs. Environment: The Twin Equation 125
- Cognition and Perception: The Brain as Interpreter 125
- Plasticity: The Brain Can Change 125
- When Biology Becomes Vulnerability 125
- Reflection Exercise 126
- Summary 126

Chapter 9: Personality in Context: Culture, Upbringing, and Society 127
- Introduction 127
- Upbringing: The First Laboratory of Personality 127
- Culture: The Invisible Personality 127
- Socioeconomic and Educational Influences 127
- Learned Helplessness: When Environment Teaches Powerlessness 128
- Breaking the pattern: 128
- Social Conditioning and Conformity 128
- The Feedback Loop of Society and Self 129
- Reflection Exercise 129
- Summary 129

Chapter 10: Growth and Change: How Personality Evolves Across the Lifespan ... 130
- Introduction 130
- The Lifespan Arc of Personality 130
- Therapy and Self-Awareness: The Catalyst of Change 130
- Resilience and Post-Traumatic Growth 130
- The Role of Reflection and Meaning 131
- Aging and the Personality Curve 131
- Choice, Habit, and Freedom 131
- Reflection Exercise 131
- Summary 131

Appendices
Appendix A: Attachment Theory: How Early Bonds Shape Personality 132
- Introduction 132
- The Core Idea: The Need for a Secure Base 132
- The Four Primary Attachment Styles 132

- Attachment and the Adult Personality 134
- The Neurobiology of Attachment 134
- Healing Insecure Attachment 134
- Reflection Exercise 135
- Summary 135

Appendix B: Cognitive Biases, Logical Fallacies, and Thinking Errors 136
- Introduction 136
- Section 1: Cognitive Biases – The Mind's Shortcuts 136
- Section 2: Logical Fallacies – The Art of False Persuasion 137
- Section 3: Thinking Errors in Everyday Life 139
- Section 4: Strategies for Avoiding Biases and Fallacies 139
- Reflection Exercise 140
- Summary 140

Appendix C: Emotional Intelligence and Regulation 141
- Introduction 141
- The Five Pillars of Emotional Intelligence 141
- The Physiology of Emotion Regulation 141
- Healthy vs. Unhealthy Emotional Reactions 142
- Developing Emotional Regulation Skills 143
- Empathy and Boundaries 143
- Reflection Exercise 144
- Summary 144

Appendix D: Somatic Awareness and the Mind–Body Connection 145
- Introduction 145
- The Nervous System: A Brief Overview 145
- Common Physical Expressions of Emotional States 145
- Body Posture and Emotional Feedback 146
- Practical Grounding Sequence 147
- Reflection Exercise 147
- Summary 147

Final Section: A Note of Caution and Responsibility 148
Resources and Crisis Help 149
- United States (National): 149
- If you are outside the United States: 149
- If you are in immediate danger: 149

References
- General Mental Health and Personality 150
- Mood and Emotional Disorders 151
- Neurodevelopmental Conditions (Autism, ADHD) 151

Obsessive-Compulsive and Related Disorders...........................152
Psychotic and Thought Disorders...................................152
Trauma and Stressor-Related Disorders..............................152
General Psychology and Brain Science...............................153
Appendix A: Attachment Theory.....................................153
Appendix B: Cognitive Biases, Logical Fallacies, and Thinking Errors.........153
Appendix C: Emotional Intelligence and Regulation.......................154
Appendix D: Somatic Awareness and the Mind–Body Connection............154

The Modern Mindset

Foreword

We live in an age of relentless noise: news, opinions, advice, and explanations for everything. Yet despite all that noise, most people still wrestle with the same quiet questions: *Why do I react this way? Why do I feel this strongly? Why can't I seem to change?*

This workbook was written to answer those questions—not with slogans or quick fixes, but with understanding. *The Modern Mindset* is a guided exploration of how personality, emotion, and habit shape the way we move through the world. It blends respected psychological theory with practical exercises, reflection prompts, and clear explanations, helping you see yourself with sharper accuracy and greater compassion.

The material is organized into three major parts, followed by a set of practical appendices. Each section builds on the last, gradually connecting personality, emotion, and behavior into a single, coherent picture of what it means to be human.

Part I: Personality and Type

This section introduces the core framework of the book—the sixteen personality types derived from Jungian theory. It explains how preferences for thinking, feeling, intuition, and perception form recognizable patterns in behavior.

Each type is presented with depth and honesty: its strengths, blind spots, emotional habits, and common career or relationship patterns. You'll learn that these types are not boxes but languages—ways to articulate your natural tendencies and those of others.

By the end of Part I, you'll understand how temperament influences decision-making, communication, and even how we handle conflict or affection.

Part II: Personality and Mental Health

Part II bridges temperament with psychology. It examines how personality traits interact with mental and emotional well-being. Topics include the distinction between personality and personality disorder; how anxiety, depression, and trauma distort self-perception; and how compassion replaces judgment when we understand behavior as adaptation.

This section clarifies terms often misused in popular culture—*narcissist*, *psychopath*, *depression*, *OCD*—and grounds them in proper psychological meaning. It's not a diagnostic guide, but a translation manual for understanding the emotional diversity around us.

You'll learn how to recognize patterns of thought and feeling, where personality ends and disorder begins, and when professional help is the right path forward.

Part III: Personality in Context

This part widens the lens. It explores how culture, upbringing, and social environment shape personality expression. Here you'll find discussions of learned helplessness, social conditioning, resilience, and growth across the lifespan.

Part III shows that personality isn't fixed; it's responsive. Reflection, therapy, and lived experience can reshape the mind's habits. You'll see how the self evolves—maturing from reaction to awareness, from instinct to intention.

Appendices: Practical Frameworks for Growth

The appendices expand on the tools introduced throughout the book, turning abstract theory into practical application.

Appendix A explains Attachment Theory: how early relationships form the blueprint for adult intimacy and trust.

Appendix B outlines Cognitive Biases and Logical Fallacies that cloud clear thinking and decision-making.

Appendix C introduces Emotional Intelligence and practical methods for regulating emotion, with examples of healthy versus unhealthy reactions to everyday challenges.

Appendix D explores Somatic Awareness—how the body mirrors emotion and how posture, breath, and physical presence can guide the mind back to calm.

Together, these appendices create a toolbox for daily use: how to listen to yourself, reason clearly, and stay balanced under stress.

What You'll Gain

This book isn't about changing who you are; it's about seeing who you are with clarity. You'll learn to:

- Identify your personality type and understand its real-world implications.
- Recognize emotional and cognitive habits that shape your daily choices.
- Communicate more effectively by understanding the patterns behind others' behavior.
- Develop emotional regulation and empathy without losing boundaries.
- Approach conflict, uncertainty, and growth with steadier confidence.

By the end, you'll have a working vocabulary for self-understanding and a set of tools for practical change. The theories you'll encounter—Jungian typology, attachment, emotional intelligence, and cognitive bias—represent centuries of psychology distilled into one usable framework.

The mind isn't a mystery to be solved but a system to be understood. *The Modern Mindset* invites you to step into that understanding calmly, curiously, and with the respect that every thinking, feeling human being deserves.

Notes on Attribution

This workbook is based on the personality typology originally described by Carl Jung and later developed by Katharine Cook Briggs and Isabel Briggs Myers.

The Myers–Briggs Type Indicator® and MBTI® are registered trademarks of The Myers & Briggs Foundation, which has neither reviewed nor endorsed this material.

The Myers–Briggs Type Indicator®, Myers–Briggs®, MBTI®, and the MBTI® logo are trademarks or registered trademarks of The Myers & Briggs Foundation, Inc., and The Myers & Briggs Company. This publication is an independent work and has not been reviewed or endorsed by either organization.

Preface

This book was born out of both frustration and hope.

Frustration, because the language of psychology has escaped its original purpose. Words like *narcissist*, *sociopath*, *OCD*, or *depressed* are now tossed around social media as insults or excuses, stripped of their meaning and precision.

Hope, because beneath that noise, people are still trying to understand themselves and others. The intent is there—it simply needs better tools.

I wrote *The Modern Mindset* as a kind of corrective: a bridge between sound psychological knowledge and everyday life. You don't need a degree to grasp how your mind works, but you do need structure, honesty, and restraint. This workbook was designed to give you all three.

Why This Book Exists

The world is full of reaction. Anger, division, and confusion dominate both public and private life, much of it born not from malice but from misunderstanding. We misread intentions. We mistake personality for morality. We interpret someone's fear or avoidance as hostility. We judge others by their behavior but ourselves by our motives.

Our culture urgently needs better mental health, stronger coping skills, and a deeper grasp of why people do what they do—including ourselves. We spend years learning mathematics, grammar, and history, yet few of us ever learn how to interpret the signals of our own mind. We're taught *how* to think, but not *how we think*.

That's what this book tries to fix.

What This Book Is and Isn't

This is a workbook for self-understanding, not a diagnostic manual. It can help you see patterns of thought and emotion, but it cannot tell you who you are in any absolute sense. Human beings are fluid.

Personality frameworks such as the MBTI or Keirsey's Temperament Theory describe recurring tendencies; they do not define character or limit potential.

I've also included sections on mental health conditions and emotional regulation. These aren't here so readers can play doctor—they're here because people deserve accurate language for their own experiences. When you can name something correctly, you can deal with it more honestly.

Still, this material is not a substitute for therapy. If you recognize yourself in descriptions of depression, trauma, or anxiety, take that as a signal to seek help, not as proof of a diagnosis. Professionals exist for a reason: they have both the training and the distance required to help safely. No workbook, however thorough, can replace that.

And while self-reflection is vital, restraint is just as important. Resist the urge to use this material to label others. You cannot see inside another person's mind. You can observe patterns, but you cannot read motives. True understanding requires consent, curiosity, and humility.

Why the Appendices Exist

The appendices grew out of the same intention: to repair the tools we use for thinking and coping.

Attachment Theory because so many relational struggles trace back to learned safety or fear.

Cognitive Biases and Logical Fallacies because clear thinking is the foundation of mental health; self-deception can harm as much as anxiety.

Emotional Intelligence because awareness without empathy becomes arrogance.

Somatic Awareness because the body is the first and last witness to emotion—understanding it is part of healing.

Each of these sections is meant to restore balance to how we see ourselves: logical yet compassionate, self-critical yet forgiving, mindful yet practical.

What You Will Gain

This workbook will not change your life in a single read. What it will do is help you understand why your life unfolds the way it does, and how to adjust course with greater skill. You'll gain vocabulary for self-reflection, insight into others' behavior, and practical ways to calm the emotional reflexes that drive conflict.

If you approach this book with sincerity, you'll come away with more than knowledge. You'll come away with clarity—the rarest commodity in an age of distraction.

Project Purpose

This project is, at its heart, a defense of reason and empathy—two traits often in short supply, yet indispensable for civilization and personal peace alike. If more people understood how their own minds worked, we might have less cruelty, less division, and fewer broken conversations.

The purpose of *The Modern Mindset* is not to perfect anyone. It's to make self-awareness a normal skill and compassion a logical consequence of understanding.

So take your time with these pages. Read slowly. Reflect often. Apply what fits, and question everything else.

How to Use This Workbook

The Modern Mindset is not meant to be read once and shelved. It is designed to be used, revisited, and applied. Think of it as a guided exploration—part textbook, part mirror, and part field manual for being human.

Understanding yourself is not a single moment of revelation; it is a process of repeated noticing: how you think, how you react, and how you choose. Each time you return to these pages, you'll see something new—not because the text has changed, but because you have.

The Workbook Format

You'll encounter sections of explanation followed by short reflection prompts or exercises. These are not optional flourishes; they are the bridge between information and transformation. Reading without reflection turns knowledge into trivia. Writing, thinking, and practicing are what turn it into self-awareness.

Use a notebook, journal, or the margins of the book itself to record your answers. No one else needs to see them. Honesty matters more than eloquence.

If an exercise feels uncomfortable, slow down. Discomfort is usually a sign that you've touched something true.

Why the MBTI Comes First

The book begins with personality typology—specifically the Myers–Briggs Type Indicator (MBTI) and its Jungian foundation—for a simple reason: you can't understand emotion or behavior without first understanding how your mind is built to perceive and decide.

Each MBTI type represents a habitual pattern of attention and reasoning. It reveals whether you tend to act from instinct (gut and emotion) or intellect (analysis and reflection), and how you naturally balance the two.

Learning your type is not about classification or limitation; it's about identifying your default settings—the mental shortcuts your brain uses when life demands a quick response. Once you recognize those instincts, you gain the freedom to question them. You start to see the difference between what feels natural and what is wise.

That distinction—between reflex and reason—is the essence of emotional maturity. The MBTI section gives you the foundation for every chapter that follows. Emotional regulation, mental bias, attachment, and even somatic awareness all build upon your basic cognitive habits.

How to Read the Book

You may read the book straight through or move between sections that feel most relevant. For a first read, though, follow the sequence. Each part builds upon the last.

- **Part I** helps you understand how you process information and decide what matters.
- **Part II** connects those patterns to mental health and emotional balance.
- **Part III** expands your perspective to environment, culture, and growth over time.
- **The Appendices** give you practical methods for thinking clearly, relating deeply, and regulating emotion.

Once you've completed the book, revisit earlier sections. Self-awareness evolves with context; the insights you gain later will reshape how you understand the first chapters.

Using the Exercises

Every exercise is an opportunity to experiment. Don't skip them, even when they seem simple. Writing down your answers anchors abstract thought in physical reality; it slows the mind enough to watch it working.

You may find that repeating an exercise months later yields a different result. That isn't inconsistency—it's growth. Use each prompt as a snapshot of your mindset at a given moment. Collect them like data points in the ongoing study of yourself.

The Spirit of the Work

Approach this book as both scientist and subject: curious, disciplined, but compassionate. No one gets this perfectly right. Self-awareness is a lifelong experiment conducted in real time.

The goal isn't to "fix" yourself; it's to understand why you are the way you are—so that when you act, you do so with intention, not compulsion.

Read slowly. Reflect often. Revisit freely. The more times you return, the more the material becomes part of how you see, not just what you know.

In short:

- Don't rush.
- Don't skim.
- Don't skip the exercises.
- And most importantly, don't treat personality as a cage.

Understanding your type is the beginning of freedom.

The Architecture of Personality

A Brief History of Understanding the Mind

The effort to classify human behavior is as old as thought itself. Long before laboratories and fMRI scans, philosophers and physicians were already trying to explain why one person is cautious while another is reckless, one tender and another aloof. The story of personality theory is really the story of psychology becoming a science: a slow transition from myth to method, from intuition to evidence.

From Temperament to Type

The first great system of personality came from Hippocrates in the fifth century B.C.E. and was refined by Galen centuries later. They proposed the four temperaments—sanguine, choleric, melancholic, and phlegmatic—each supposedly caused by the balance of bodily humors: blood, yellow bile, black bile, and phlegm.

Primitive biology aside, the idea that mood and behavior follow consistent, observable patterns was revolutionary. These temperaments remained influential for nearly two millennia, shaping medicine, literature, and early psychology.

During the Renaissance, philosophers began linking temperament to the soul rather than the body. Descartes separated mind and matter, while Locke suggested that experience formed personality through learning. Yet the language of temperament survived well into the nineteenth century, reborn as an interest in character—a moral rather than medical concept.

Psychology Becomes a Science

By the late 1800s, psychology was moving out of philosophy and into laboratories. Wilhelm Wundt founded the first experimental psychology lab in 1879 in Leipzig, measuring reaction times and sensory thresholds. His student William James brought psychology to the United States, writing *The Principles of Psychology* (1890), which described consciousness as a flowing "stream" rather than fixed compartments.

At the same time, Sigmund Freud developed psychoanalysis, proposing that unconscious drives—not conscious reason—direct much of human behavior. Freud's model of the id, ego, and superego was less experiment than theory, but it introduced the idea that personality could be understood as an internal structure with moving parts—a psychological architecture.

Freud's contemporaries splintered from him but retained his fascination with inner structure. Carl Jung emphasized the self's innate drive toward wholeness and proposed psychological types based on how individuals gather information (sensation versus intuition) and make decisions (thinking versus feeling). Alfred Adler focused on power and inferiority, while Karen Horney emphasized social and cultural influence. Collectively, they shifted the focus from pathology to pattern.

From Typology to Measurement

The first real personality tests emerged in the early twentieth century, propelled by the need to classify soldiers during World War I. The Woodworth Personal Data Sheet (1917) was a rudimentary questionnaire designed to identify "neurotic" recruits. It paved the way for self-report inventories—structured lists of statements rated for truth or frequency.

In 1943, Katharine Cook Briggs and her daughter Isabel Briggs Myers adapted Jung's typology into a practical instrument: the Myers–Briggs Type Indicator (MBTI). Their goal was not diagnosis but understanding—to help people find suitable careers and improve communication by recognizing differing cognitive preferences. The MBTI distilled Jung's ideas into four dichotomies:

- Extraversion / Introversion
- Sensing / Intuition
- Thinking / Feeling
- Judging / Perceiving

Combinations of these yielded sixteen recognizable patterns. While modern psychologists debate its scientific rigor, its enduring popularity lies in accessibility—it gives people language for tendencies they already sense.

Parallel developments continued in academia. Raymond Cattell's factor analysis produced the 16 PF test. Hans Eysenck identified three key dimensions: Extraversion, Neuroticism, and Psychoticism. Eventually, statistical consensus produced the Five-Factor Model—Openness, Conscientiousness, Extraversion, Agreeableness, and Neuroticism—which remains the dominant research framework today.

Where the MBTI maps preferences, the Big Five measures traits along continua. Both describe the same territory from different altitudes.

The Broader History of Psychiatry and Psychology

As typology matured, psychiatry evolved from asylum medicine into neuroscience. Early psychiatrists like Emil Kraepelin categorized mental illnesses, laying the groundwork for today's *Diagnostic and Statistical Manual of Mental Disorders* (DSM).

In the mid-twentieth century, behaviorism dominated. Figures like John B. Watson and B.F. Skinner reduced behavior to stimulus and response, treating personality as secondary.

But the pendulum soon swung back with humanistic psychology—Carl Rogers, Abraham Maslow, and others—who argued that people are not machines but meaning-seeking beings capable of growth. Personality became the bridge between biology, cognition, and philosophy.

Today, modern psychology integrates all of these threads. Neuroscience studies brain structure; clinical psychology studies disorder; personality psychology studies pattern; and positive psychology studies potential. Together they form the scaffolding for any serious look at human behavior.

Why This History Matters

Knowing this lineage prevents misuse. Typologies and inventories were never meant to reduce people to letters or numbers; they were designed to make reflection possible. Each generation of psychology refined the same question: *How much of what I do is instinct, and how much is reason?*

Personality frameworks like the MBTI sit at that intersection. They help reveal when we act automatically—guided by temperament or emotion—and when we pause to choose deliberately. Recognizing those patterns does not trap you; it helps you understand the architecture of your own mind—the blueprint that shapes decisions, relationships, and growth.

Looking Ahead

In the pages that follow, you'll encounter the sixteen personality types and the cognitive dynamics that animate them. Treat them as maps, not verdicts. A map shows where you tend to go; it doesn't dictate where you must remain.

Understanding your type is the first step toward mastering the balance between impulse and intention, between instinct and intellect—the balance that defines the modern mindset.

Part I: Understanding the Myers–Briggs Type Indicator (MBTI)

The Origin of the System

The early twentieth century was a period of intense experimentation in the human sciences. Physicists were redefining the universe, while psychologists were attempting to redefine the self. Freud had already opened the door to the unconscious, but his focus on pathology—repression, trauma, and libido—left many thinkers searching for a model that explained not just illness but difference.

Why do two equally healthy minds perceive the same event so differently? Why does one person find meaning in logic and another in empathy? The emerging field of psychological typology tried to answer that.

Jung's Insight: The Machinery of the Mind

Swiss psychiatrist Carl Gustav Jung believed that human consciousness is not a blank slate but a structured system—a set of natural preferences for how we take in information and make decisions. He described these preferences as psychological functions: sensation, intuition, thinking, and feeling.

In Jung's model, each person naturally leans toward one way of perceiving and one way of judging. Sensation notices what *is*—the tangible, measurable facts. Intuition grasps what *could be*—the unseen pattern beneath events. Thinking decides by logic and consistency, while feeling decides by values and impact on others.

None of these functions are superior; they simply represent different modes of navigation. Every person uses all four, but one typically dominates, supported by a secondary, a tertiary, and a least-developed ("inferior") function. The tension among these parts gives the psyche both balance and conflict.

Jung also proposed the key dimension of introversion and extraversion, not as social behavior but as the direction of psychic energy—whether attention flows inward to reflection or outward to engagement. Combined with the four functions, this produced eight core orientations of mind.

He saw these not as labels but as living dynamics. "Every individual," he wrote, "is an exception to the rule." The purpose of typology was not to divide humanity into boxes but to make sense of its astonishing variety.

From Theory to Practical Application

Jung's ideas were complex and metaphorical. They explained the mind's architecture beautifully, yet they were difficult to apply outside the consulting room.

Decades later, Katharine Cook Briggs and her daughter Isabel Briggs Myers sought to translate Jung's system into something practical—a way for ordinary people to understand their psychological preferences without psychoanalytic training.

They refined Jung's eight functions into four measurable dichotomies: Extraversion vs. Introversion, Sensing vs. Intuition, Thinking vs. Feeling, and Judging vs. Perceiving. From these, they produced sixteen recognizable combinations that form the foundation of the Myers–Briggs Type Indicator (MBTI).

A Tool for Understanding, Not Judgment

Briggs and Myers intended the MBTI as a mirror, not a verdict. It was designed to foster empathy in workplaces, families, and classrooms—to show that people differ not in intelligence or morality but in method. Where one person seeks data, another seeks meaning; where one values principle, another values harmony.

When used correctly, the MBTI remains one of the simplest ways to visualize the interplay between instinct and intellect—how you process, decide, and react when the world demands action.

First published in 1962, the MBTI has since become one of the most widely used personality frameworks in the world. Today it is employed by psychologists, educators, corporations, military organizations, and counselors for career guidance, team-building, and personal development.

The Four Core Dichotomies

Every personality type in the MBTI system is built from four paired preferences, like four sliding scales that describe how you tend to move through the world. These are not moral judgments or fixed categories; they simply show where your mind goes first when it has a choice. With self-awareness and practice, you can use both sides of each spectrum.

1. Extraversion (E) / Introversion (I)

Where energy is directed: outward toward people and activity, or inward toward reflection and thought.

Extraversion and introversion describe not social skill but the flow of psychological energy. Extraverts draw vitality from interaction; they think best through dialogue and activity, often discovering what they believe as they speak. The external world of people, projects, and events recharges them. Silence and solitude, while tolerable, can feel draining after a while.

Introverts, by contrast, draw energy from their inner world of ideas and impressions. They think best in quiet, form opinions internally before expressing them, and need recovery time after too much stimulation. Their calm exterior often hides a rich mental life.

Neither approach is superior. Extraverts risk acting before reflecting; introverts risk reflecting so long they never act. Both need balance—a rhythm of engagement and retreat—to remain healthy.

2. Sensing (S) / Intuition (N)

How information is gathered: through concrete facts and details, or through abstract patterns and meanings.

Sensing types trust what they can see, touch, and verify. They notice details, remember specifics, and prefer practical information that can be acted upon. They focus on the present moment, valuing tradition, precision, and proven methods.

Intuitive types look beyond the literal. They see connections, implications, and possibilities. They focus on what might be rather than what is. They are drawn to theories, symbolism, and big-picture thinking. Their strength lies in imagination and foresight, though they may sometimes overlook immediate realities others find essential.

Sensing provides stability; intuition provides innovation. Every society, and every balanced individual, needs both—the builders who notice each stone and the visionaries who imagine the cathedral.

3. Thinking (T) / Feeling (F)

How decisions are made: by logic and objective analysis, or by empathy and personal values.

Thinkers evaluate situations using fairness, logic, and consistency. They ask, "What makes sense? What's true regardless of who it affects?" They value clarity, debate, and justice. In conflict, they seek resolution through facts and rational structure, even when it feels impersonal. Their challenge is remembering that logic, though fair, can sometimes feel cold.

Feelers, by contrast, evaluate situations through emotional impact and human context. They ask, "What matters most to the people involved? What feels right?" They prize empathy, harmony, and compassion, and they tend to avoid harsh criticism or discord. Their strength is understanding emotion; their risk is sacrificing fairness or boundaries to preserve peace.

Thinking builds systems; feeling builds trust. Mature decision-making requires both—the heart to care and the reason to choose wisely.

4. Judging (J) / Perceiving (P)

How life is approached: with structure and closure, or with flexibility and openness to change.

Judging types prefer order, schedules, and closure. They like to plan ahead, meet deadlines, and follow through. Structure gives them peace of mind, not because they fear change but because they function best when life feels organized and predictable. Their motto might be "Work first, relax later."

Perceiving types thrive in spontaneity. They like open options, enjoy adapting to change, and often find inspiration in improvisation. They resist rigid plans because too much structure feels stifling. Their motto might be "Let's see where this goes."

Judging types bring reliability; perceivers bring adaptability. Each has a blind spot: the J type can become controlling under stress, while the P type can drift into indecision. Maturity lies in knowing when to commit and when to remain open.

In sum:

- Extraversion and Introversion show where your energy comes from.
- Sensing and Intuition reveal how you perceive the world.
- Thinking and Feeling shape how you make decisions.
- Judging and Perceiving describe how you live those decisions out.

Together, these four preferences create the framework of your cognitive style—the architecture of your personality. They explain not what you believe but *how* you believe.

Who Uses the MBTI and Why

The MBTI remains popular because it translates complex psychological theory into practical insight.

Businesses use it to improve communication, leadership, and conflict resolution.

Educators use it to tailor learning environments.

Counselors and coaches use it to help clients understand strengths, motivations, and blind spots.

Individuals use it for self-reflection—to identify natural tendencies, potential careers, and ways to grow.

While the MBTI has critics (notably among academic psychologists who favor evidence-based models like the Big Five), its descriptive power makes it valuable when used thoughtfully rather than dogmatically.

Other Major Personality Frameworks

The MBTI is one of several modern systems that attempt to map human personality. Among the most recognized are:

- **The Big Five (OCEAN)**: a research-based model describing five broad traits—Openness, Conscientiousness, Extraversion, Agreeableness, and Neuroticism.
- **The Enneagram**: a nine-type system focused on core motivations and emotional defense patterns.
- **DISC**: emphasizing behavioral tendencies—Dominance, Influence, Steadiness, and Compliance.
- **Temperament Theory (Keirsey)**: a simplified model grouping MBTI types into four "temperaments": Guardians, Artisans, Idealists, and Rationals.

Each framework highlights different aspects of personality. None are absolute; all are lenses through which to interpret behavior and preference.

Alternate Personality Frameworks Explained

Modern personality theory has evolved along several paths. While the Myers–Briggs system is the most familiar to general audiences, other models highlight different aspects of what makes people distinct. Each framework has its strengths, limitations, and unique vocabulary. Together, they show that personality can be examined from multiple angles—behavioral, emotional, social, and cognitive.

1. Temperament Theory (Keirsey)

Psychologist David Keirsey built on the Myers–Briggs typology by grouping the sixteen MBTI types into four temperaments, each representing a broad motivational pattern. His model focuses less on abstract mental processes and more on observable behavior—how people act, communicate, and prioritize in real life.

- **Artisan (SP)**: spontaneous, adaptable, driven by excitement and hands-on skill.
- **Guardian (SJ)**: dependable, organized, tradition-oriented, and community-minded.
- **Idealist (NF)**: empathic, value-driven, focused on personal growth and authenticity.
- **Rational (NT)**: analytical, strategic, independent, and inventive.

Keirsey viewed these temperaments as recurring patterns throughout history—ancient archetypes of human interaction that offer a lens for understanding social roles, work habits, and leadership styles.

2. The Big Five Personality Model (OCEAN)

The Big Five, or Five-Factor Model, represents the current scientific consensus in personality psychology. Derived from decades of empirical research and statistical analysis, it describes personality across five broad, measurable dimensions:

- **Openness to Experience** — curiosity, creativity, and comfort with novelty.

- **Conscientiousness** — organization, discipline, and reliability.
- **Extraversion** — sociability, energy, and assertiveness.
- **Agreeableness** — empathy, kindness, and cooperation.
- **Neuroticism** — sensitivity to stress and emotional instability.

Unlike typological systems that divide people into categories, the Big Five measures personality along continuous scales. You can be moderately open, highly conscientious, or low in neuroticism. It is the most widely used framework in psychological research because it is both quantifiable and predictive of real-world outcomes, from job performance to relationship satisfaction.

3. The Enneagram of Personality

The Enneagram combines spiritual and psychological traditions, blending introspection with motivation theory. It describes nine core personality types, each organized around a central fear and desire that shape thought and behavior:

- **The Reformer** — principled and perfection-seeking.
- **The Helper** — caring and approval-oriented.
- **The Achiever** — success-driven and image-conscious.
- **The Individualist** — expressive and identity-focused.
- **The Investigator** — analytical and detached.
- **The Loyalist** — security-seeking and cautious.
- **The Enthusiast** — adventurous and pleasure-driven.
- **The Challenger** — assertive and control-oriented.
- **The Peacemaker** — calm and harmony-seeking.

Each type connects to two "wings" (adjacent types) and can shift under stress or growth. The Enneagram's value lies in its focus on motivation and emotion—it helps explain *why* people act, not just *how* they act.

4. Socionics

Developed in Eastern Europe during the 1970s by Lithuanian researcher Aushra Augustinavičiūtė, Socionics expands on Jung's cognitive theory and the MBTI framework but introduces a new concept: **information metabolism**—the idea that personality types differ in how they process and exchange information.

Socionics identifies sixteen types like the MBTI but focuses on **intertype relations**—how two people's types interact dynamically. It predicts compatibility, communication ease, and sources of tension. Where MBTI focuses on individual cognition, Socionics studies the social system of personalities as if they were interlocking gears.

Its terminology and structure are complex, but the model is valuable for understanding group dynamics, teamwork, and relational chemistry in greater depth than most Western frameworks attempt.

Perspective

Each of these systems describes personality from a different angle:

- Keirsey captures everyday temperament.
- The Big Five measures stable traits scientifically.
- The Enneagram explores inner motivation and emotion.
- Socionics analyzes interpersonal dynamics and compatibility.

Together, they remind us that no single theory owns the truth of human nature. Each adds a layer of insight to the intricate architecture of personality.

For readers who wish to explore further:

David Keirsey's *Please Understand Me II* remains the best introduction to Temperament Theory.

The Big Five is summarized in accessible form through university psychology departments and studies archived by the American Psychological Association and the National Institutes of Health.

The Enneagram Institute provides reliable descriptions and self-assessments for the nine types.

English-language resources for Socionics are maintained by Socionics.com and academic sites focused on information processing theory.

Each framework can complement your understanding of MBTI by revealing a different dimension of how people think, feel, and relate.

Interpreting MBTI: Your Type

Learning your type is only the beginning. The value of typology lies not in the letters themselves, but in what they reveal about the rhythm of your mind—how you take in the world, make sense of it, and act on that understanding.

Each of the sixteen types represents a distinct balance of energy, perception, judgment, and lifestyle preference. These patterns influence everything from your communication style to your emotional reflexes, yet none of them determine your fate. Your type is a description of tendency, not destiny.

Think of it as the default setting on a complex instrument. Knowing that default allows you to play it deliberately rather than by accident.

The Four-Letter Code

The four-letter code (for example, INFP or ESTJ) is a shorthand summary of your cognitive habits. Each letter represents one preference from the four dichotomies introduced earlier:

- **E** or **I** – where you direct your energy: outward or inward.
- **S** or **N** – how you gather information: through facts or intuition.
- **T** or **F** – how you make decisions: through logic or empathy.
- **J** or **P** – how you structure your outer life: orderly or flexible.

Together, they form a type that describes both *how you think* and *how you appear* to others. Yet beneath those four letters lies a dynamic process of mental interaction known as the **function stack**—the sequence of cognitive preferences that shape perception and decision-making.

Cognitive Functions: The Engine Beneath the Surface

Every type contains a hierarchy of mental functions: a dominant, auxiliary, tertiary, and inferior. These are not skills to acquire but habits of attention—ways your mind automatically filters experience.

Jung described eight total functions, combining the four basic processes (thinking, feeling, sensation, intuition) with the two directions of energy (introversion or extraversion). The result is a map of how the psyche prioritizes information:

- Extraverted Thinking (Te) – organizing the external world through logic and efficiency.
- Introverted Thinking (Ti) – analyzing internal models of consistency and accuracy.
- Extraverted Feeling (Fe) – attuning to others' emotions and social harmony.
- Introverted Feeling (Fi) – aligning choices with inner values and authenticity.
- Extraverted Intuition (Ne) – exploring ideas, connections, and possibilities.
- Introverted Intuition (Ni) – perceiving patterns, symbols, and long-range meaning.
- Extraverted Sensing (Se) – immersing in immediate physical experience.
- Introverted Sensing (Si) – recalling detail, precedent, and internalized memory.

Each personality type relies most heavily on two of these functions—the dominant and the auxiliary. The first gives confidence and energy; the second balances and supports it. The tertiary and inferior functions develop later, often surfacing under stress or through maturity.

For example, an **INTJ** leads with Introverted Intuition (Ni) supported by Extraverted Thinking (Te). They trust abstract insight but validate it with evidence and structure. Under pressure, their inferior function, Extraverted Sensing (Se), can appear suddenly—causing them to overindulge in sensory distractions or become overly focused on the moment.

Conversely, an **ESFP** leads with Extraverted Sensing (Se) and supports it with Introverted Feeling (Fi). They thrive on real-world engagement, acting spontaneously while guided by strong internal values. Their opposite, Introverted Intuition (Ni), often develops slowly and provides wisdom only after experience.

Understanding these internal mechanisms transforms the MBTI from a label into a language.

Type Dynamics

The four letters describe *what* you prefer; the function stack explains *how* those preferences work in motion. Two people with the same letters may still differ in maturity, awareness, and emotional control, depending on how balanced their functions are.

Healthy individuals develop their auxiliary function to balance the dominant one. An Extravert who lives entirely in outer activity without introspection becomes scattered; an Introvert who stays in endless thought without outward engagement becomes detached. The same principle applies to Sensing and Intuition, Thinking and Feeling, Judging and Perceiving. Growth means learning to use the neglected side when the situation calls for it.

For that reason, your MBTI type should be viewed as a starting point for integration, not a fixed identity.

The Shadow Functions

The lesser-used four functions—your "shadow"—operate unconsciously. They appear in dreams, projection, stress responses, or moments of extreme emotion. They are not villains but mirrors, revealing the parts of yourself you least understand or most avoid.

A logical type may suddenly act emotionally; a feeling type may become coldly analytical. These reversals often happen when the psyche is overworked or when a person is forced into unfamiliar circumstances. Learning to recognize the shadow reduces its control.

Carl Jung called this process *individuation*: the gradual integration of the conscious and unconscious self. It is not about becoming someone else; it is about becoming whole.

How to Read Type Descriptions

When you explore your MBTI type in the chapters that follow, remember that the descriptions are tendencies, not commandments. They illustrate common traits, not destiny. Use them to identify patterns in thought, communication, and stress response.

If something feels slightly inaccurate, that's expected. Your environment, education, and trauma history can all influence expression. Type describes potential, not the totality of experience.

A helpful approach is to read both your own type and those of close friends, partners, or colleagues. You'll begin to see that many conflicts are not moral at all—they are linguistic. People simply speak different cognitive dialects.

Purpose of Typology

The ultimate goal of typology is empathy through understanding. Once you grasp how different people process the same event in fundamentally different ways, judgment gives way to curiosity.

Typology teaches humility: that your way of perceiving is not *the* way but *a* way. It allows for self-acceptance without self-indulgence and compassion without naivety.

If you finish this section knowing not only what your type is but how it *works*, you will already be ahead of most who treat personality as entertainment. The rest of the book will build on this insight—linking your cognitive habits to emotional regulation, relationships, and mental health.

A Word of Caution: Understanding vs. Labeling

It is tempting to treat personality types as boxes—to use them as shortcuts for judgment rather than tools for understanding. That temptation is natural; the human mind craves order. But personality theory, when used carelessly, can become the very thing it was meant to prevent: reductionism.

Labels simplify, but they also distort. Once we call someone an *INTJ* or an *ESFP*, we risk seeing only the pattern and not the person. The mind that built these categories also built biases; it loves to predict, categorize, and assume. The responsible use of typology requires discipline—the ability to hold knowledge without letting it harden into stereotype.

When you encounter someone whose type differs from yours, avoid the impulse to treat that difference as a flaw. A thinker's precision is not coldness; a feeler's empathy is not weakness; a sensor's practicality is not lack of imagination; an intuitive's abstraction is not detachment from reality. Each represents a valid cognitive approach to life.

The goal of studying typology is not to classify but to clarify. It gives you language for describing patterns that already exist within you and around you. The purpose is empathy—first for yourself, then for others.

Every personality theory, no matter how refined, is a map, not a mirror. A map shows structure and relation; it cannot capture the landscape's color, light, or motion. Likewise, MBTI and its relatives can help you orient yourself in the psychological terrain, but they cannot replace the experience of living it.

If you ever catch yourself using a type as an excuse ("That's just how I am") or as a weapon ("You always do that because you're a..."), pause. You have stopped using typology as understanding and started using it as armor. Awareness should liberate, not limit.

Understanding is an act of humility. Labeling is an act of control. The difference between the two is not intellectual—it is moral.

Discovering Your Type

The Myers–Briggs Type Indicator (MBTI) describes sixteen personality types, each defined by four paired preferences:

- **Extraversion (E) vs. Introversion (I):** how you direct energy—outward or inward.
- **Sensing (S) vs. Intuition (N):** how you gather information—through facts or patterns.
- **Thinking (T) vs. Feeling (F):** how you make decisions—by logic or by values.
- **Judging (J) vs. Perceiving (P):** how you approach structure—organized or adaptable.

Each pairing combines into a four-letter type code that captures your natural pattern of focus, perception, and decision-making.

Here are the sixteen types with concise characterizations:

- ISTJ – **The Inspector:** responsible, detail-oriented, and dutiful.
- ISFJ – **The Protector:** loyal, thoughtful, and committed to helping others.
- INFJ – **The Counselor:** idealistic, insightful, and driven by meaning.
- INTJ – **The Mastermind:** strategic, independent, and perfectionistic.
- ISTP – **The Crafter:** practical, analytical, and skilled at hands-on problem-solving.
- ISFP – **The Composer:** gentle, adaptable, aesthetic, and values personal freedom.
- INFP – **The Healer:** introspective, empathetic, and guided by inner ideals.
- INTP – **The Architect:** curious, theoretical, and seeks logical coherence.
- ESTP – **The Dynamo:** energetic, spontaneous, and thrives on action and results.
- ESFP – **The Performer:** outgoing, lively, and enjoys the moment and connection with others.
- ENFP – **The Champion:** imaginative, passionate, and drawn to possibility and cause.
- ENTP – **The Visionary:** inventive, quick-witted, and loves debate and innovation.
- ESTJ – **The Supervisor:** efficient, structured, and prefers clear rules and systems.
- ESFJ – **The Provider:** sociable, caring, and skilled at organizing people and events.
- ENFJ – **The Teacher:** charismatic, empathetic, and driven to inspire and lead.
- ENTJ – **The Commander:** assertive, decisive, and naturally gifted at planning and leadership.

Each type represents a recurring pattern of mental energy and decision-making, not a box. MBTI is descriptive rather than predictive; it shows how people tend to operate, not what they can or cannot do.

Self-Assessment: Discovering Your Preferences

This reflection exercise helps you identify your natural tendencies. There are no points or scores—only patterns. Answer honestly rather than aspirationally; the goal is awareness, not idealization.

1. Extraversion (E) vs. Introversion (I)

Ask yourself:

- When you need to recharge, do you prefer **being around people and activity**, or **quiet and solitude**?
- Do you often **think out loud to process ideas**, or **think privately before sharing**?
- When making plans, do you favor **spontaneous gatherings** or a **small, familiar circle**?
- In conversation, do you usually **speak first and refine later**, or **listen first and respond after reflecting**?

If your answers lean toward **energy from interaction**, you favor **Extraversion (E)**.
If they lean toward **energy from reflection**, you favor **Introversion (I)**.

2. Sensing (S) vs. Intuition (N)

Ask yourself:

- When learning, do you focus more on **facts and details**, or on **patterns and concepts**?
- Do you trust **direct experience**, or do you rely more on **hunches and possibilities**?
- Are you more comfortable describing **what is**, or speculating about what **could be**?
- Do you enjoy **step-by-step methods**, or **big-picture brainstorming**?

If you rely on what is **real**, **tangible**, and **verifiable**, you favor **Sensing (S)**.
If you rely on **insight**, **abstraction**, and **future possibilities**, you favor **Intuition (N)**.

3. Thinking (T) vs. Feeling (F)

Ask yourself:

- When making decisions, do you focus on **logic and consistency**, or on **values and human impact**?
- Is it more important to be **fair and objective**, or **compassionate and considerate**?
- When resolving conflict, do you seek **principled reasoning**, or **emotional understanding**?

- Do you prefer feedback that is **blunt and factual**, or **tactful and encouraging**?

If your answers emphasize **detached analysis**, you favor **Thinking (T)**.
If they emphasize **human context** and **empathy**, you favor **Feeling (F)**.

4. Judging (J) vs. Perceiving (P)

Ask yourself:

- Do you like to **plan ahead and stick to schedules**, or **stay flexible and adapt as things unfold**?
- When finishing tasks, do you **feel relief when it's done early**, or **when it's done right, even if late**?
- Do you prefer **clear structure and closure**, or **open options and spontaneity**?
- Does an unexpected change **annoy you**, or **excite you**?

If you value **organization**, **deadlines**, and **decisiveness**, you favor **Judging (J)**.
If you value **openness**, **adaptability**, and **exploration**, you favor **Perceiving (P)**.

Interpreting Your Type

Combine one letter from each pair:

- **E or I** – where you get energy.
- **S or N** – how you take in information.
- **T or F** – how you make decisions.
- **J or P** – how you approach structure.

For example, someone who gains energy alone (I), focuses on ideas (N), decides by logic (T), and prefers flexibility (P) would be **INTP**, often called *The Architect*.

Your combination points to a pattern, not a prescription. It describes your mental habits—the way your attention naturally moves through the world. As you read the upcoming chapters, you'll see how those letters translate into real strengths, blind spots, and styles of growth.

Compatibility Notes

Compatibility patterns in MBTI describe how different types tend to interact based on shared values, communication styles, and decision-making preferences. These patterns reflect general tendencies, not fixed rules. Two highly compatible types can still struggle if communication breaks down, and two seemingly challenging types can thrive when they understand each other's needs. These compatibility tiers help readers anticipate areas of natural ease, mutual growth, or possible friction. They are meant to guide awareness, not dictate outcomes. Healthy relationships, romantic or platonic, depend more on maturity, communication, and respect than on type alone.

ISTJ – The Inspector

Core Traits

The ISTJ personality type—*Introverted, Sensing, Thinking, Judging*—embodies steadiness, responsibility, and an unshakable respect for structure. These individuals prefer order to chaos, rules to guesswork, and reliability to novelty.

ISTJs tend to take life seriously. They feel a moral obligation to do things properly, not because they crave praise, but because order itself feels right. They approach life methodically, relying on precedent and logic more than speculation. When others panic, they keep their heads.

Their quiet confidence comes from experience; their focus, from integrity. The result is a personality that holds families, workplaces, and communities together—often without being noticed until they're gone.

Cognitive Overview

- **Dominant:** Introverted Sensing (Si) – stores and recalls detail, tradition, and precedent to maintain stability.
- **Auxiliary:** Extraverted Thinking (Te) – organizes the outer world logically and efficiently.
- **Tertiary:** Introverted Feeling (Fi) – forms private moral convictions and empathy that mature over time.
- **Inferior:** Extraverted Intuition (Ne) – brings occasional flashes of creativity and speculation, often under stress or during growth.

This blend produces the archetypal "Inspector": cautious yet competent, practical yet moral. They find reassurance in what is proven, but maturity teaches them to value innovation when it serves function and principle.

Temperament as a Child

ISTJ children crave structure and dependability. They like clear rules, steady routines, and consistent authority figures. They learn best from predictable adults who reward follow-through and honesty. Praise that acknowledges reliability ("You kept your word") motivates them more than emotional appeals.

They may appear shy or cautious at first, preferring to observe before joining group play. Abrupt changes—new teachers, chaotic classrooms, or shifting family routines—can cause quiet distress. Providing schedules, explanations, and stability helps them thrive.

Over time, gentle encouragement to take calculated risks strengthens their adaptability and prepares them for the unpredictable parts of adulthood.

Temperament as an Adult

As adults, ISTJs exude calm competence. They value hard work, rules, and clear responsibilities. They become the reliable core of institutions—those who ensure the plan is followed, the books are balanced, and promises are kept.

Their independence is often misunderstood. ISTJs rarely seek attention and may appear emotionally reserved, but their loyalty runs deep. They express affection through duty, acts of service, and consistency.

Under stress, their perfectionism can surface as rigidity or pessimism. They may worry about potential failures and resist untested ideas. Rest, solitude, and trusted routines help them reset.

Best Learning Style

ISTJs learn best through structured instruction, clear expectations, and measurable results. They prefer practical examples over abstract theories. Step-by-step learning with immediate feedback suits them well.

They excel in subjects that reward precision and procedure: mathematics, science, finance, medicine, law, or engineering. When lessons connect to real-world use, retention soars. They appreciate mentors who are organized, factual, and competent.

Open-ended brainstorming or ambiguous goals frustrate them unless anchored by tangible objectives.

Workplace Habits

At work, ISTJs are reliable, disciplined, and efficient. They honor the chain of command and expect others to meet their obligations. When given autonomy, they thrive—so long as the expectations are clear.

They respect tradition but will improve systems if logic demands it. Change must be justified with evidence, not enthusiasm. Once convinced, they implement new methods with quiet excellence.

They prefer environments where rules are enforced, tasks are concrete, and productivity is measured by results. Feedback should be specific, constructive, and framed as improvement rather than criticism.

Common ISTJ careers include law enforcement, accounting, civil service, medicine, engineering, and military administration—fields that demand accountability and precision.

Friendships

ISTJs form friendships carefully but deeply. They value dependability, honesty, and shared values more than spontaneity or emotional display. They may not initiate often, but once connected, they remain loyal for years.

They are practical friends—more likely to help fix your car or review your résumé than to offer poetic advice. Their affection is shown through reliability, not grand gestures.

They respect boundaries and expect others to do the same. Flakiness or dishonesty can end a friendship abruptly, as they view integrity as nonnegotiable.

Love Life

ISTJs approach relationships with seriousness and loyalty. They see love as a promise, not an experiment.

They express affection through commitment, stability, and service rather than overt romance. To them, consistency is intimacy. They value partners who are dependable, pragmatic, and emotionally grounded.

Arguments are approached like problems to solve. While they can appear detached during conflict, their goal is resolution, not distance. They may struggle with overly emotional or impulsive partners who expect constant reassurance.

When paired with someone who values their steadiness and honors their integrity, ISTJs make profoundly devoted life partners.

Money Management

Financial prudence comes naturally to ISTJs. They budget meticulously, save consistently, and prefer security over risk. Long-term planning—retirement funds, home ownership, and insurance—brings peace of mind.

They dislike debt and impulsive spending. Investments are usually conservative and research-based. They may struggle to spend on leisure or luxury, viewing it as frivolous unless tied to practical value.

At their best, they are excellent stewards of resources—measured, cautious, and responsible. Their challenge is remembering that money can also serve comfort and joy, not just survival and order.

Best Parts of the Type

- Dependable in every sense of the word—if they say it, they mean it.
- Possess strong moral integrity and an instinct for fairness.
- Masterful at logistics, systems, and practical problem-solving.
- Provide emotional and financial stability to others.
- Quietly resilient; rarely panic in crisis.
- Maintain high standards for themselves and their environment.

Worst Parts of the Type

- Can become rigid or dismissive of new methods.
- May suppress emotions until they surface as irritation or exhaustion.
- Often struggle to delegate, believing others won't meet their standards.
- Risk becoming judgmental toward those seen as careless or inconsistent.

- Under stress, may catastrophize minor changes or lose perspective on what truly matters.

Growth and Development

For ISTJs, growth means learning flexibility and trust in possibility. Their inferior Extraverted Intuition (Ne) can feel like chaos, but embracing it opens new horizons. They benefit from occasional spontaneity—trying new experiences without needing to perfect them.

Emotionally, developing their Introverted Feeling (Fi) helps them connect values to empathy. When they express their convictions instead of just enforcing rules, their wisdom gains warmth and influence.

At full maturity, ISTJs become living examples of balanced order—stable yet open-minded, principled yet compassionate, disciplined yet human.

ISTJ Compatibility

Friendship

High: ISFJ, ESFJ, ISTP
Moderate: ISTJ, ESTJ, INTJ, INTP
Challenging: ENFP, ENTP, ENFJ, ESFP, ESTP, INFJ, INFP, ENTJ

Romantic

High: ISFJ, ESFJ, ESTJ
Moderate: ISTJ, INTJ, ISTP
Challenging: ENFP, ENFJ, ENTP, ESFP, ESTP, INFJ, INFP, ENTJ

ISFJ – The Protector

Core Traits

The ISFJ personality type—*Introverted, Sensing, Feeling, Judging*—is defined by quiet dedication and deep empathy. Often described as "the protector" or "the nurturer," ISFJs combine warmth with discipline. They are generous with their time, patient with others' needs, and quietly proud of fulfilling their obligations.

These individuals balance compassion with structure. They are sentimental yet practical, sensitive yet steadfast. ISFJs often become the caretakers of families, communities, and institutions, ensuring that others are safe, supported, and remembered.

They value tradition and stability, not from rigidity but from a belief that order protects people. Where others might see duty as burden, the ISFJ sees it as love in action.

Cognitive Overview

- **Dominant:** Introverted Sensing (Si) – records and recalls detailed experiences, creating a strong internal sense of continuity and responsibility.
- **Auxiliary:** Extraverted Feeling (Fe) – senses the emotional needs of others and acts to maintain harmony.
- **Tertiary:** Introverted Thinking (Ti) – supports logic and structure, allowing emotional insight to be expressed practically.
- **Inferior:** Extraverted Intuition (Ne) – sparks imagination and speculation but may appear as anxiety under stress.

This function stack makes ISFJs empathetic realists. They care deeply, but they also act methodically, ensuring their compassion translates into stability rather than chaos.

Temperament as a Child

ISFJ children are gentle, observant, and eager to please. They thrive in structured environments with consistent expectations. Teachers often describe them as conscientious and kind.

They are naturally attuned to the emotional climate of the home. Discord or harsh criticism can wound deeply. Encouragement and routine allow their sense of security and confidence to grow.

As children, they may struggle to express anger or disappointment, preferring to internalize conflict. Parents can help them by validating feelings and teaching that assertiveness is not rudeness—it is self-respect.

Temperament as an Adult

As adults, ISFJs become pillars of dependability. They are meticulous in duty, loyal to family, and attentive to details others overlook. They often work behind the scenes, ensuring the world runs smoothly while avoiding the spotlight.

They have a gift for remembering personal details—birthdays, anniversaries, favorite meals—and use this information to express care. Their relationships are grounded in service and reliability.

Under stress, ISFJs may feel unappreciated or overwhelmed by the weight of others' needs. They tend to overextend themselves, saying yes when they should rest. Recharging through solitude, nature, or quiet reflection helps restore balance.

Best Learning Style

ISFJs learn best through structured, sequential instruction that connects directly to real-life usefulness. They excel when they understand how a lesson will benefit others or serve a larger purpose.

They are patient learners who prefer a calm environment, practical examples, and steady guidance. Repetition and visual memory reinforce knowledge effectively.

Abstract theories may feel disconnected unless linked to tangible outcomes. When teachers or mentors provide encouragement and clear standards, ISFJs flourish.

Workplace Habits

At work, ISFJs are conscientious, dependable, and people-oriented. They are the colleagues who quietly ensure tasks are completed and that everyone is treated fairly.

They respect hierarchy, prefer defined roles, and find comfort in order. ISFJs excel in positions that blend structure with compassion—nursing, teaching, administration, social work, or human resources.

They dislike conflict and may absorb others' stress to preserve peace. Leaders can best support ISFJs by giving clear expectations, consistent feedback, and personal acknowledgment of their contributions.

Friendships

ISFJs make loyal, gentle friends who show affection through small acts of care—checking in, remembering milestones, offering practical help. They are dependable listeners who provide emotional steadiness during turmoil.

They prefer deep, long-term friendships to wide social circles. Their trust builds slowly but endures once earned. They take others' feelings seriously and may struggle when friends act inconsiderately or forget commitments.

Because they internalize hurt, ISFJs benefit from friends who encourage open discussion and remind them that boundaries are healthy.

Love Life

In love, ISFJs are tender, sincere, and steadfast. They show affection through service—acts of kindness, daily reliability, and quiet devotion. Grand romantic gestures mean less to them than consistency and respect.

They seek stable, long-term partnerships built on mutual care. Their ideal relationship feels like teamwork rather than drama.

ISFJs sometimes neglect their own needs while caring for others. They may stay too long in imbalanced relationships out of loyalty. A supportive partner helps them express needs clearly and recognize that self-care strengthens love rather than diminishes it.

Money Management

ISFJs are cautious and practical with money. They prefer security over risk and plan for long-term stability. Saving for emergencies or family needs brings them peace of mind. They are generous but not reckless, often spending on others' comfort before their own. They dislike debt and tend to live within their means.

Their main financial challenge is learning to spend occasionally on personal enjoyment without guilt. When balanced, they handle resources with prudence and compassion.

Best Parts of the Type

- Deeply loyal and protective of loved ones
- Remarkably dependable and detail-oriented
- Possess strong memory and organizational skill
- Show care through action rather than words
- Empathetic and intuitive about others' emotional states
- Bring harmony and stability to any environment

Worst Parts of the Type

- Overextend themselves by taking on too much responsibility
- Struggle to say no or ask for help
- May suppress anger or sadness until it becomes exhaustion
- Can become resentful if their efforts go unacknowledged
- Risk defining self-worth entirely by service to others
- Under stress, may catastrophize or retreat into self-criticism

Growth and Development

ISFJs grow most when they learn to balance service with self-care. Their instinct to help others is admirable, but unchecked it can lead to fatigue and quiet resentment. Setting boundaries and recognizing their own needs prevents burnout.

Developing their tertiary Introverted Thinking helps them analyze objectively and separate emotion from duty. Cultivating their inferior Extraverted Intuition encourages flexibility and confidence when facing change.

As ISFJs mature, they evolve from protectors of people to wise guardians of values—offering empathy, stability, and grace to a world that often forgets both.

ISFJ Compatibility

Friendship

High: ISTJ, ESFJ, ISFP
Moderate: ISFJ, INFJ, INFP, ESTJ
Challenging: ENTP, ENFP, ENTJ, ESTP, ESFP, ENFJ, INTJ, ISTP

Romantic

High: ISTJ, ESFJ, ISFP
Moderate: INFJ, INFP, ISFJ
Challenging: ENTP, ENFP, ENTJ, ESTP, ESFP, ENFJ, INTJ, ESTJ

INFJ – The Counselor

Core Traits

The INFJ personality type—*Introverted, Intuitive, Feeling, Judging*—is known for depth, empathy, and vision. INFJs seek meaning in everything they do. They are introspective idealists who combine insight with conviction, seeing life not as a series of events but as a story of purpose.

They intuitively read people's emotions and motivations, often perceiving what others cannot articulate. Beneath their calm exterior lies a passionate sense of mission—to heal, teach, guide, or improve the world in quiet, lasting ways.

Though soft-spoken, INFJs possess inner strength. They balance imagination with structure and prefer depth over breadth in relationships, ideas, and experiences.

Cognitive Overview

- **Dominant:** Introverted Intuition (Ni) – perceives patterns, underlying meanings, and long-term implications.
- **Auxiliary:** Extraverted Feeling (Fe) – senses emotional dynamics and fosters harmony.
- **Tertiary:** Introverted Thinking (Ti) – organizes thoughts logically and clarifies abstract concepts.
- **Inferior:** Extraverted Sensing (Se) – anchors them in the physical present, though often underdeveloped or ignored.

The INFJ's dominant intuition allows them to see how small details connect to larger truths. Their auxiliary feeling translates those insights into empathy and action. The combination gives them the rare gift of understanding both *why* people struggle and *how* to help.

Temperament as a Child

INFJ children are imaginative, observant, and sensitive to others' emotions. They may prefer solitary play, fantasy worlds, or creative projects that allow them to express ideas symbolically.

They notice subtle cues—tone, expression, tension in a room—and often act as emotional barometers for family or classmates. When praised for creativity and kindness, they thrive. When dismissed or criticized harshly, they may withdraw deeply.

They need reassurance that their inner world has value. Adults should encourage their imagination but also teach boundaries, helping them understand that not every feeling they sense must be absorbed or fixed.

Temperament as an Adult

As adults, INFJs become thoughtful, principled individuals who often dedicate themselves to causes greater than themselves. They are natural counselors, teachers, writers, and advocates. They want to make a difference, but in personal, human-scale ways rather than through power or attention.

They are private yet warm, calm yet determined. They think long before speaking but speak with precision when they do. They can appear mysterious to others because their decisions are based on internal clarity, not external logic.

When unhealthy or overburdened, INFJs may withdraw, overanalyze, or absorb others' pain until they burn out. Solitude, art, nature, and meaningful conversation restore their balance.

Best Learning Style

INFJs learn best through conceptual exploration tied to human meaning. They are motivated by understanding *why* something matters rather than by rote memorization.

They excel in quiet, reflective environments where they can engage deeply with ideas. Subjects that integrate philosophy, psychology, literature, or ethics resonate strongly.

They benefit from mentors who inspire curiosity and connect theory to values. Their learning solidifies when they can express insights creatively—through writing, dialogue, or visual symbolism.

Workplace Habits

In the workplace, INFJs are conscientious and purpose-driven. They seek harmony and meaning in their roles. Routine work feels empty unless it serves a larger mission.

They are excellent at mentoring, mediating, and long-term planning. They prefer structured independence—clear goals, but freedom in method.

Conflict and cynicism drain them quickly. Supportive leaders who respect their integrity and insight bring out their best work. Common careers include counseling, education, psychology, writing, art, and nonprofit leadership.

Friendships

INFJs value a few close, authentic friendships over a large social circle. They are attentive listeners who remember emotional details and provide steady emotional support.

They seek deep conversations about life, meaning, and personal growth. Superficial small talk exhausts them. They show loyalty through empathy, discretion, and presence—quietly standing by friends during difficulty.

When betrayed, they withdraw completely, finding it hard to rebuild trust. Friends who respect their privacy and reciprocate emotional honesty earn their lifelong loyalty.

Love Life

In love, INFJs are devoted, romantic, and idealistic. They look for emotional depth, shared vision, and mutual growth. They do not fall easily, but when they do, they commit wholeheartedly.

They express affection through empathy, attention, and gentle insight into a partner's needs. They crave emotional transparency but may hesitate to express their own vulnerabilities for fear of burdening others.

They may overidealize partners or expect unspoken emotional reciprocity, leading to disappointment. Healthy relationships help them balance compassion with assertiveness and remind them that love requires openness, not perfection.

Money Management

INFJs are careful, ethical, and moderate in financial matters. They view money as a means to support purpose, not as an end in itself. They often save reliably but may neglect personal comfort if they see greater moral or relational needs elsewhere.

They prefer low-risk, meaningful investments—education, travel, or charitable causes. They dislike waste and debt. Their challenge lies in learning that self-care spending is not indulgence but sustainability.

Best Parts of the Type

- Deep empathy and insight into human nature
- Visionary thinking paired with quiet discipline
- Profound emotional loyalty and discretion
- Strong sense of purpose and ethical conviction
- Natural ability to mentor, counsel, and heal others
- Creative imagination that connects ideas across disciplines

Worst Parts of the Type

- Can become perfectionistic or overidealistic
- May internalize others' pain until emotionally exhausted
- Struggle to express needs or anger directly
- Risk withdrawing into isolation when misunderstood
- Sensitive to criticism and prone to self-doubt
- Tend to overthink or overanalyze motives and outcomes

Growth and Development

INFJs grow through self-acceptance and emotional openness. Their lifelong challenge is to stop overinterpreting and start experiencing. By engaging with the present moment—through art, physical activity, or direct action—they ground their vision in reality.

Developing their inferior Extraverted Sensing helps them stay connected to life as it unfolds, while strengthening their tertiary Introverted Thinking refines their insights with logic.

When mature, INFJs become living examples of wisdom through compassion—able to see truth clearly, feel deeply, and act gently without losing strength.

INFJ Compatibility

Friendship

High: ENFP, ENTP, INFP
Moderate: INFJ, INTJ, ISFJ, ESFJ
Challenging: ISTJ, ESTJ, ESTP, ESFP, ENTJ, ISTP

Romantic

High: ENFP, ENTP, INFP
Moderate: INFJ, INTJ
Challenging: ISTJ, ESTJ, ESTP, ESFP, ENTJ, ISTP, ESFJ, ISFJ

INTJ – The Mastermind

Core Traits

The INTJ personality type—*Introverted, Intuitive, Thinking, Judging*—is analytical, independent, and relentlessly strategic. Often described as "the architect of ideas," INTJs possess a deep drive to understand complex systems and improve them. They prefer logic over tradition and competence over popularity.

They live in a world of patterns and possibilities, constantly seeking to understand how things work and how they could work better. Efficiency is their native language; inefficiency, their greatest frustration. Behind their calm and often serious exterior lies a mind that is constantly mapping, forecasting, and refining.

INTJs rarely speak without purpose. Their ideas are precise, their goals deliberate, and their methods structured. They are both visionaries and engineers—designers of systems that outlast them.

Cognitive Overview

- **Dominant:** Introverted Intuition (Ni) – focuses on abstract patterns, long-term implications, and strategic foresight.
- **Auxiliary:** Extraverted Thinking (Te) – organizes the external world with logic, structure, and results-oriented action.
- **Tertiary:** Introverted Feeling (Fi) – forms private moral convictions and a quiet sense of authenticity.
- **Inferior:** Extraverted Sensing (Se) – experiences the present moment but may overwhelm or distract them when under stress.

This cognitive architecture produces a mind both visionary and precise—one that plans for decades but acts with cold efficiency in the present.

Temperament as a Child

INTJ children are observant, curious, and self-directed. They tend to prefer solitary play, building complex systems or narratives rather than engaging in group activities. Adults often describe them as "little adults," with a seriousness and independence uncommon for their age.

They dislike busywork and are frustrated by rules that make no logical sense. When given freedom to explore interests deeply, they flourish. However, emotional overexposure or unpredictable environments may lead them to retreat into their private worlds.

They thrive when teachers and parents respect their autonomy, reward competence, and explain *why* rules exist instead of insisting on blind obedience.

Temperament as an Adult

As adults, INTJs embody purposeful focus. They set long-term goals and methodically build toward them, often becoming experts or innovators in their chosen fields. They are natural planners, preferring mastery over multitasking and depth over breadth.

They are confident in their reasoning but skeptical of authority. They trust systems and data more than emotion or tradition. Their blunt honesty can unsettle those who equate politeness with agreement.

INTJs often appear reserved, but beneath that restraint lies intense passion for ideas and integrity. They can work alone for long stretches, but they value competent partners and colleagues who challenge them intellectually.

Best Learning Style

INTJs are conceptual learners who thrive on autonomy. They absorb information best when allowed to connect it to broader frameworks or future applications. Abstract theories and complex systems fascinate them.

They resist rote memorization or shallow exercises. A strong mentor or structured challenge ignites their focus. They retain knowledge through synthesis—by applying ideas across disciplines.

They learn best when left to pursue mastery independently, but they appreciate clear objectives and logical standards of performance.

Workplace Habits

In professional environments, INTJs are strategic, efficient, and often ahead of their peers. They prefer long-term planning to short-term reaction and thrive in positions that reward independent thinking and problem-solving.

They dislike inefficiency, redundant meetings, or emotional decision-making. Their communication is direct and pragmatic, often stripped of unnecessary social polish.

They make exceptional leaders when they remember that others need emotional context, not just direction. They command respect through competence and vision, not charm. Common INTJ careers include science, engineering, research, strategy, management, architecture, and law.

Friendships

INTJs form few friendships, but those they keep are meaningful and lasting. They gravitate toward people who are intelligent, reliable, and capable of independent thought.

They value intellectual companionship over emotional display. Friends who take offense easily or require constant reassurance may exhaust them. Once trust is established, however, INTJs are fiercely loyal and protective, offering pragmatic advice and honest insight.

They often prefer deep one-on-one conversations to group socializing. For them, friendship means mutual respect and growth, not constant contact.

Love Life

In relationships, INTJs are committed, private, and pragmatic. They seek partners who respect their independence and intellect rather than those who demand emotional theatrics.

They express affection through consistency, problem-solving, and support for a partner's goals. They rarely engage in casual romance and view commitment as a deliberate choice.

Their challenge is learning to verbalize emotions. Because they feel deeply but communicate rationally, they can appear detached even when fully devoted. Partners who appreciate stability, honesty, and loyalty often find INTJs deeply rewarding companions.

Money Management

INTJs approach money with logic and foresight. They plan for long-term security and efficiency, viewing finances as another system to optimize. Budgets, investments, and contingency funds are second nature.

They are neither miserly nor reckless—simply strategic. They prefer delayed gratification over impulse. Risk is calculated, not avoided. They tend to invest in education, technology, or ventures that promise growth rather than status.

Their main challenge is remembering that financial control should serve quality of life, not replace it.

Best Parts of the Type

- Visionary thinking paired with practical execution
- High personal integrity and self-discipline
- Exceptional strategic foresight and planning ability
- Independent, confident, and capable of sustained focus
- Logical yet deeply principled decision-making
- Calm in crisis, able to see long-term consequences clearly

Worst Parts of the Type

- Can appear cold, distant, or overly critical
- Impatient with inefficiency or emotional reasoning
- Tendency toward perfectionism and unrealistic self-expectations
- Difficulty delegating or trusting others' competence
- May suppress feelings until they manifest as irritation or withdrawal
- Under stress, may fixate on control and reject feedback

Growth and Development

INTJs grow by learning empathy and adaptability. Their greatest strength—strategic clarity—can become rigidity when unchecked. Developing their inferior Extraverted Sensing helps them engage with the present instead of only forecasting the future.

Allowing emotion and spontaneity to coexist with reason deepens their wisdom. By balancing intellect with vulnerability, they evolve from detached strategists into wise visionaries capable of both insight and connection.

At full maturity, INTJs embody quiet mastery: deliberate, thoughtful, and fiercely committed to truth—an ideal blend of mind and will.

INTJ Compatibility

Friendship

High: ENTP, ENFP, INTP
Moderate: INTJ, INFJ, ISTJ, ENTJ
Challenging: ESFP, ESTP, ESFJ, ISFJ, ESTJ, ISTP

Romantic

High: ENFP, ENTP, INTP
Moderate: INTJ, INFJ
Challenging: ESFP, ESTP, ESFJ, ISFJ, ESTJ, ISTP, ENTJ

ISTP – The Crafter

Core Traits

The ISTP personality type—*Introverted, Sensing, Thinking, Perceiving*—is pragmatic, curious, and self-reliant. Known as "The Crafter" or "The Virtuoso," ISTPs are the hands-on problem-solvers of the world. They prefer direct engagement with reality—disassembling, testing, and rebuilding until they understand how something truly works.

These individuals have an innate grasp of mechanics, physics, and motion. They're not theorists; they're tinkerers, experimenters, and troubleshooters. They value freedom over conformity and precision over pretense. Where others deliberate endlessly, ISTPs take action.

They live in the present moment, reacting quickly and skillfully to changing circumstances. Independence is not a preference—it's a necessity.

Cognitive Overview

- **Dominant:** Introverted Thinking (Ti) – analyzes systems for internal logic and consistency.
- **Auxiliary:** Extraverted Sensing (Se) – engages with the physical world in real time, responding swiftly and accurately.
- **Tertiary:** Introverted Intuition (Ni) – offers occasional flashes of abstract insight and pattern recognition.
- **Inferior:** Extraverted Feeling (Fe) – seeks harmony and connection but often remains underdeveloped or expressed indirectly.

This configuration produces a personality that is analytical yet spontaneous, calm under pressure yet restless in routine. The ISTP mind is always asking, "How does this work—and how can it work better?"

Temperament as a Child

As children, ISTPs are inquisitive and observant, often drawn to objects rather than words. They enjoy taking things apart—gadgets, toys, machines—to understand their workings. They prefer learning through direct experience, not explanation.

They resist excessive supervision and dislike being told what to do "just because." When adults allow them to explore safely, they become inventive and confident. When restricted or micromanaged, they withdraw or rebel.

They benefit from practical challenges, freedom to experiment, and adults who explain the "why" behind rules instead of enforcing them blindly.

Temperament as an Adult

Adult ISTPs value autonomy and competence. They are decisive in crisis but relaxed otherwise. They dislike bureaucracy, small talk, and emotional overexposure. Instead, they thrive in environments where skill matters more than politics.

They are masters of improvisation—mechanics who can repair an engine with minimal tools, surgeons who stay calm under pressure, or athletes who instinctively adjust mid-play.

They are not naturally sentimental, but their loyalty is deep once earned. ISTPs live by quiet principles of fairness and respect, and they despise hypocrisy or melodrama.

Best Learning Style

ISTPs learn by doing. They need direct engagement—tools in hand, data on screen, or physical examples to analyze. Lectures and abstractions bore them unless tied to tangible outcomes.

They excel in vocational, technical, and applied-science settings. Once they understand a concept, they test it immediately, experimenting until it works in practice.

They retain information best when allowed to manipulate, modify, and apply it. Theoretical discussion without utility feels meaningless to them.

Workplace Habits

In the workplace, ISTPs are resourceful and efficient. They cut through clutter to solve immediate problems. They thrive in environments that reward skill, precision, and independence.

They resist unnecessary rules and prefer to be judged by results rather than procedures. Pressure energizes them—crisis situations often bring out their best.

Their leadership style is pragmatic: they lead by example, not authority. They respect competence and expect the same from others. Common ISTP careers include engineering, emergency response, surgery, law enforcement, mechanics, and technical trades.

Friendships

ISTPs are loyal but private friends. They prefer a few trusted companions over a crowd. They value shared activities—hiking, building, fixing, or competing—more than long emotional discussions.

They show affection through action rather than words. When a friend needs help, an ISTP will quietly appear, fix the issue, and leave without asking for thanks.

They dislike clinginess, manipulation, or needless drama. Friendship, to them, is about mutual respect and freedom to be oneself.

Love Life

In love, ISTPs are steady, adaptable, and loyal—once they commit. They are cautious with emotion, preferring to show affection through presence and action rather than declarations.

They value partners who are independent, competent, and emotionally low-maintenance. They dislike being smothered or controlled and need personal space to recharge.

They can appear detached during conflict, but that detachment allows them to stay logical. They focus on solutions, not arguments. Their challenge lies in expressing vulnerability rather than fixing everything in silence.

Money Management

ISTPs treat money as a practical tool. They are neither extravagant nor miserly but prefer flexibility and immediate utility over long-term accumulation.

They spend on equipment, experiences, or hobbies that improve skill and efficiency. They dislike rigid budgeting but are surprisingly good at maintaining financial balance when left to their own systems.

Their main risk is impulsive spending during boredom or stress. When they view money as a resource for freedom and learning, their financial stability remains strong.

Best Parts of the Type

- Calm and effective in emergencies
- Naturally skilled at troubleshooting and repair
- Independent, adaptable, and unflappable under stress
- Value honesty and directness over social pretense
- Combine analytical reasoning with real-world practicality
- Capable of deep focus and technical mastery

Worst Parts of the Type

- Impatient with inefficiency or emotional excess
- Can withdraw emotionally when bored or pressured
- Resist authority or long-term commitments they find restrictive
- Struggle to articulate feelings, leading others to misread their intentions
- May take unnecessary risks for stimulation
- Under stress, may act impulsively or isolate themselves completely

Growth and Development

ISTPs grow through emotional awareness and foresight. Their mastery of the present moment can make them neglect long-term consequences. Learning to anticipate effects—financial, relational, or emotional—turns instinct into wisdom.

Developing their inferior Extraverted Feeling helps them express care openly and navigate social nuance without discomfort. Cultivating patience and self-reflection strengthens their influence and connection with others.

At full maturity, ISTPs become balanced craftsmen of life itself—decisive but thoughtful, free yet responsible, grounded in the moment while aware of the future.

ISTP Compatibility

Friendship

High: ESTP, ISFP, INTP
Moderate: ISTP, ISTJ, ESFP, ESTJ
Challenging: ENFJ, ENFP, INFJ, ENTJ, ESFJ, ISFJ, INTJ

Romantic

High: ISFP, ESTP, INTP
Moderate: ISTP, ESFP
Challenging: ENFJ, ENFP, INFJ, INTJ, ESFJ, ISFJ, ENTJ, ESTJ, ISTJ

ISFP – The Composer

Core Traits

The ISFP personality type—*Introverted, Sensing, Feeling, Perceiving*—is gentle, artistic, and independent. Often called "The Composer" or "The Artist," ISFPs live through their senses and values rather than theories or traditions. They are quiet observers of beauty—drawn to color, texture, movement, and mood—and they express what they feel more easily through action or art than through speech.

They are sensitive but not fragile. Beneath their calm, accommodating exterior lies a resilient spirit that refuses to live dishonestly. They crave authenticity and freedom: to be themselves, to follow what feels right, and to create harmony in their surroundings without conforming to expectation.

They seek lives rich in experience and emotion—less about achievement and more about *meaning*.

Cognitive Overview

- **Dominant:** Introverted Feeling (Fi) – builds an internal moral compass based on deeply held personal values.
- **Auxiliary:** Extraverted Sensing (Se) – engages vividly with the present moment and the beauty of sensory experience.
- **Tertiary:** Introverted Intuition (Ni) – provides occasional insights and direction toward deeper purpose.
- **Inferior:** Extraverted Thinking (Te) – applies structure and logic when absolutely necessary but feels restrictive.

This combination gives ISFPs a unique emotional intelligence—they feel everything intensely but quietly, acting with empathy and sincerity rather than drama. Their decisions come from conscience, not consensus.

Temperament as a Child

ISFP children are affectionate, sensitive, and imaginative. They enjoy tactile and creative play—drawing, building, exploring nature, or interacting with animals. They are typically easygoing, though easily hurt by harsh words or criticism.

They learn best through experience and emotional connection. A caring tone and gentle encouragement motivate them far more effectively than discipline or rigid control.

Because they are conflict-averse, they may suppress frustration to maintain peace. Teaching them that it's safe to express emotions directly helps them develop resilience and confidence.

Temperament as an Adult

As adults, ISFPs are empathetic, loyal, and quietly adventurous. They follow their own rhythm, preferring work and relationships that align with personal meaning rather than external reward. They dislike pretense and avoid competitive or manipulative environments.

They are natural aesthetes—drawn to careers or hobbies that involve design, music, cooking, craftsmanship, or nature. They often express love through thoughtful gestures and acts of service rather than speeches or analysis.

While they value harmony, they are also fiercely independent. If their freedom or integrity is threatened, they may disappear without warning, choosing solitude over forced conformity.

Best Learning Style

ISFPs learn best through **hands-on, emotionally relevant experiences**. They absorb information through observation and practice rather than lecture or theory.

They thrive in creative environments that allow flexibility, personal expression, and sensory engagement. Art, music, design, health care, and environmental studies all align with their natural curiosity and compassion.

They disengage when learning feels abstract, competitive, or devoid of emotional meaning. Encouragement and personal feedback bring out their strongest work.

Workplace Habits

At work, ISFPs are conscientious, adaptable, and team-oriented when the environment feels supportive. They prefer practical, people-centered tasks to managerial roles.

They are excellent at roles requiring empathy and attention to detail—such as health care, design, teaching, or counseling. They work quietly but effectively, taking pride in craftsmanship and the human side of service.

They dislike rigid hierarchies and bureaucratic micromanagement. A respectful, collaborative atmosphere that values individuality brings out their best work.

Friendships

ISFPs are kind, loyal, and sensitive friends. They connect deeply through shared experiences and unspoken understanding rather than constant conversation. They are often the emotional anchors in their social circles—steady, kind, and quietly perceptive.

They give without expectation and value sincerity above all. However, they withdraw from relationships that feel controlling, judgmental, or insincere. They need friendships where both honesty and gentleness coexist.

Their empathy sometimes leads to emotional fatigue; learning to set boundaries keeps their kindness sustainable.

Love Life

ISFPs are tender and devoted partners who show love through presence and thoughtful action. They are attentive to small details—a favorite song, a preferred meal, a gentle touch—and express care by making life beautiful for their partner.

They crave emotional connection but dislike drama. They prefer intimacy built on mutual trust, quiet moments, and shared authenticity.

They can struggle to verbalize feelings and may retreat during conflict to avoid saying something they regret. They need partners who respect their need for reflection and encourage open dialogue without pressure.

For the ISFP, love means safety, respect, and the freedom to be genuine.

Money Management

ISFPs view money as a means of living well, not accumulating wealth. They are generous and often spend on experiences, aesthetics, or loved ones. They prefer flexibility over strict budgeting but typically maintain balance through practicality rather than calculation.

They dislike debt and extravagance but may impulsively spend when emotionally inspired or under stress. Their financial growth improves when they learn to plan for long-term security without feeling restricted.

When balanced, they manage finances with quiet wisdom—grounded in modesty, mindfulness, and appreciation for life's simple pleasures.

Best Parts of the Type

- Deeply empathetic and compassionate
- Naturally artistic and sensitive to beauty
- Gentle, adaptable, and accepting of others
- Value authenticity and emotional honesty
- Calm and steady in crisis
- Capable of remarkable kindness and selflessness

Worst Parts of the Type

- Struggle with confrontation or self-assertion
- Can internalize hurt and withdraw instead of addressing it
- May appear indecisive or disorganized when stressed
- Avoid planning ahead, leading to occasional chaos
- Overextend emotionally, neglecting their own needs
- Under pressure, may act impulsively or disappear emotionally

Growth and Development

Growth for ISFPs lies in self-assertion and foresight. Their compassion is powerful, but without boundaries it becomes exhaustion. Learning to say no and express disagreement honestly preserves their emotional energy.

Developing their inferior Extraverted Thinking helps them bring structure to their goals and follow through on long-term plans. Cultivating this function doesn't erase their spontaneity—it strengthens their independence.

As ISFPs mature, they become living examples of gentle courage: grounded in their values, guided by empathy, and unafraid to live authentically, even when the world demands conformity.

ISFP Compatibility

Friendship

High: ESFP, ISTP, ISFJ
Moderate: ISFP, INFP, ENFP, ESTP
Challenging: ENTJ, ENTP, INTJ, INFJ, ISTJ, ESTJ, ESFJ

Romantic

High: ESFP, ISTP, INFP
Moderate: ISFP, ENFP
Challenging: ENTJ, ENTP, INTJ, INFJ, ISTJ, ESTJ, ESFJ, ESTP

INFP – The Healer

Core Traits

The INFP personality type—*Introverted, Intuitive, Feeling, Perceiving*—is introspective, idealistic, and deeply empathetic. Known as "The Healer" or "The Mediator," INFPs are guided by a strong internal moral compass and a vision of how life *could* be. They are dreamers who transform reflection into creativity, compassion, and conviction.

INFPs experience emotions with remarkable intensity but often keep them private. Their lives revolve around authenticity—remaining true to who they are, even when that path feels lonely. They search for meaning, integrity, and harmony between the inner self and the outer world.

Though gentle in demeanor, they are fiercely principled beneath the surface. When something or someone violates their values, their quiet calm becomes immovable resolve.

Cognitive Overview

- **Dominant:** Introverted Feeling (Fi) – judges actions and choices according to deeply held internal values.
- **Auxiliary:** Extraverted Intuition (Ne) – explores possibilities, patterns, and creative connections.
- **Tertiary:** Introverted Sensing (Si) – recalls emotional experiences and personal lessons.
- **Inferior:** Extraverted Thinking (Te) – applies structure and order externally, often under stress or through maturity.

This function stack creates a personality that is sensitive, creative, and attuned to authenticity. INFPs look not for control, but for meaning; not for recognition, but for alignment with their inner truth.

Temperament as a Child

INFP children are imaginative, affectionate, and introspective. They often live in rich inner worlds—writing stories, daydreaming, or inventing elaborate imaginary games. They are kind-hearted and idealistic, quick to notice unfairness and eager to help those in distress.

They can be shy or overly self-critical, especially in harsh or competitive environments. Encouragement that affirms their creativity and values helps them flourish.

Criticism, on the other hand, cuts deeply; they internalize it as personal failure. They thrive when adults respect their emotional world and teach that sensitivity is a strength, not a flaw.

Temperament as an Adult

As adults, INFPs seek authenticity and purpose above all. They dislike shallow routines and jobs that conflict with their principles. They often pursue careers in counseling, writing, art, teaching, or social work—fields that allow them to express creativity and serve others meaningfully.

They are flexible in routine but unwavering in belief. They prefer harmony but will confront injustice when their conscience demands it. Their compassion runs deep, though they may struggle to translate emotion into practical action until they mature.

When overwhelmed, they may withdraw or idealize escape through fantasy, creativity, or solitude. Centering through journaling, art, or nature often restores their equilibrium.

Best Learning Style

INFPs learn best when education connects emotionally and conceptually. They need to *feel* a topic's relevance and explore it creatively. Rigid memorization bores them; discussion, exploration, and reflection engage them.

They excel at writing, languages, psychology, and the arts. They retain knowledge through storytelling, metaphor, and intuitive association. They value teachers who respect individuality and encourage personal interpretation rather than rigid conformity.

For INFPs, learning is not about accumulating facts—it is about discovering meaning.

Workplace Habits

INFPs bring empathy, creativity, and ethical awareness to the workplace. They thrive where their individuality is respected and their work aligns with their values.

They dislike authoritarian structures or constant supervision. Bureaucracy and politics drain them, while freedom and trust bring out their best. They prefer quiet environments that allow deep concentration.

They excel at creative problem-solving and conflict resolution but may struggle with deadlines or administrative minutiae. Supportive managers who provide clarity without pressure unlock their full potential.

Friendships

INFPs form friendships based on emotional connection and shared ideals. They are loyal, compassionate, and deeply invested in the well-being of those they love.

They prefer a few authentic relationships to a wide social network. They are sensitive listeners who offer perspective rather than judgment, and their presence can feel restorative to others.

However, they can become disillusioned if friends act insincerely or disregard values they hold sacred. When hurt, they often retreat into solitude rather than confront directly. Friends who appreciate their sincerity and gently encourage communication help them reemerge stronger.

Love Life

In love, INFPs are romantic idealists who crave emotional depth and authenticity. They want a partner who understands not only their words but their silences—someone who values growth, gentleness, and shared meaning over superficial attraction.

They express love through attentiveness, creativity, and emotional vulnerability. Their devotion runs deep, though they may hesitate to open up fully until trust feels absolute.

They can idealize partners, projecting inner ideals onto them, and may be disappointed when reality intrudes. Healthy relationships ground their idealism with mutual realism and emotional honesty.

For the INFP, love is both sanctuary and inspiration.

Money Management

INFPs view money as secondary to fulfillment. They prefer to spend on experiences, personal growth, and causes they believe in rather than on status or luxury.

They are often frugal out of principle but may neglect long-term planning or avoid financial discussions they find stressful. They dislike rigid budgeting yet feel anxious when funds are unstable.

They benefit from systems that automate savings and structure without suffocating spontaneity. When they learn to view financial stability as a foundation for freedom rather than constraint, they flourish.

Best Parts of the Type

- Deep empathy and emotional insight
- Creative imagination and strong sense of ethics
- Loyal, idealistic, and devoted to authenticity
- Compassionate listeners who comfort without judgment
- Naturally expressive through art, writing, or symbolic language
- Guided by conscience rather than social approval

Worst Parts of the Type

- Can be overly idealistic or self-critical
- Withdraw when hurt instead of addressing issues directly
- Struggle with practical organization or time management
- Sensitive to rejection and easily discouraged by conflict
- Risk confusing dreams with reality or avoiding decisions entirely
- Under stress, may isolate or lose motivation

Growth and Development

INFPs grow by learning to balance idealism with practicality. Their deep feelings become powerful when paired with structure and discipline. Developing their inferior Extraverted Thinking helps them turn vision into tangible results.

They benefit from setting realistic goals, accepting imperfection, and recognizing that compromise does not equal corruption. When they integrate logic with empathy, their insight gains force without losing grace.

At full maturity, INFPs embody compassionate integrity—capable of inspiring others not through authority, but through quiet conviction and unwavering humanity.

INFP Compatibility

Friendship

High: INFJ, ENFP, INTP
Moderate: INFP, INTJ, ENFJ, ISFP
Challenging: ESTJ, ISTJ, ESTP, ESFP, ENTJ, ISTP, ESFJ

Romantic

High: INFJ, ENFP, INTJ
Moderate: INFP, ENFJ
Challenging: ESTJ, ISTJ, ESTP, ESFP, ENTJ, ISTP, ENTP, ESFJ

INTP – The Architect

Core Traits

The INTP personality type—*Introverted, Intuitive, Thinking, Perceiving*—is analytical, theoretical, and endlessly curious. Known as "The Architect" or "The Thinker," INTPs are driven by a need to understand the underlying principles that govern systems, ideas, and reality itself. They live to solve puzzles, deconstruct assumptions, and build elegant frameworks of logic.

They are detached observers of life—intensely engaged in thought but often aloof in demeanor. Social conventions rarely interest them; truth does. They dislike being told *what* to think and thrive when allowed to explore *why* things work as they do.

An INTP's mind is their laboratory: abstract, dynamic, and perpetually in motion. They are the quintessential analysts and innovators who see patterns where others see noise.

Cognitive Overview

- **Dominant:** Introverted Thinking (Ti) – refines internal logic systems and seeks conceptual precision.
- **Auxiliary:** Extraverted Intuition (Ne) – generates ideas, hypotheses, and creative connections.
- **Tertiary:** Introverted Sensing (Si) – stores factual reference points and past experiences for comparison.
- **Inferior:** Extraverted Feeling (Fe) – desires social harmony but struggles with emotional expression.

This configuration creates a mind that is both critical and creative. INTPs crave intellectual freedom and are happiest when exploring open-ended questions rather than executing rigid plans.

Temperament as a Child

As children, INTPs are imaginative, independent, and fascinated by "how things work." They ask endless questions and prefer experimenting to memorizing. They are often precocious readers or inventors who value mental stimulation over social play.

They dislike arbitrary rules and may resist authority unless it makes sense to them logically. They require autonomy to explore ideas at their own pace. When misunderstood, they can retreat into books, computers, or solitary projects.

They flourish under teachers and parents who respect curiosity and provide space to think rather than demand constant conformity.

Temperament as an Adult

In adulthood, INTPs become thoughtful problem-solvers who value accuracy above all else. They prefer analysis over emotion and independence over structure. They may seem reserved, but their minds are perpetually active, synthesizing information into new theories or models.

They are often experts in their chosen domains—science, philosophy, technology, or design—yet they resist routine and bureaucratic environments. They need intellectual challenge and creative freedom to stay engaged.

When stressed, they may overanalyze to paralysis or detach from the world altogether, retreating into theory. Balance returns through physical activity, conversation with a trusted peer, or engagement in practical problem-solving.

Best Learning Style

INTPs learn best through exploration and self-directed study. They dislike rote instruction and prefer conceptual understanding over step-by-step methods. They thrive on complex problems that require independent reasoning.

They retain information by connecting new ideas to existing frameworks. They enjoy abstract subjects like philosophy, mathematics, computer science, and linguistics—fields that reward precision and originality.

They learn most effectively in environments that challenge assumptions, encourage debate, and allow intellectual autonomy.

Workplace Habits

At work, INTPs are innovative, independent thinkers who excel at analysis and troubleshooting. They are motivated by curiosity rather than hierarchy or praise. They prefer flexible schedules and minimal supervision.

They often generate groundbreaking ideas but may resist implementation or follow-up unless the problem remains intellectually engaging. Deadlines and routine tasks can feel suffocating, while freedom to explore can produce exceptional results.

They work best in roles involving research, design, strategy, or development—anything that allows theoretical depth and creative independence.

Friendships

INTPs form friendships through shared curiosity rather than emotional similarity. They enjoy exchanging ideas, debating concepts, and exploring mental challenges together.

They are loyal to those who respect their independence and intellect. While not overtly affectionate, they show care through engagement—discussing a friend's ideas, solving a problem, or offering quiet support.

They dislike emotional manipulation or excessive demands for attention. Genuine connection for an INTP means mutual understanding and intellectual honesty.

Love Life

In love, INTPs are loyal but cautious. They prefer to observe and analyze before committing, often seeking a partner who stimulates them mentally and respects their space.

They express affection subtly—through thoughtfulness, problem-solving, or philosophical conversation. Emotional displays feel uncomfortable, but once trust is established, they open deeply and sincerely.

Their challenge lies in balancing intellect with emotional responsiveness. They can unintentionally appear distant, even when they care profoundly. A patient partner who values depth over drama brings out their best.

Money Management

INTPs view money as a tool for freedom and exploration. They are typically modest in lifestyle, spending on technology, books, or hobbies rather than luxury.

They tend to neglect budgeting until necessity forces it, but their rationality helps them regain control quickly. They dislike financial risk unless it supports learning or innovation.

Their growth lies in treating financial organization not as a limitation but as a system—one more logical puzzle to master.

Best Parts of the Type

- Brilliant analytical and conceptual thinkers
- Independent, original, and deeply inventive
- Objective, fair-minded, and resistant to group pressure
- Curious about everything and unafraid of complexity
- Excellent at problem-solving and systems design
- Capable of lifelong learning and mental adaptability

Worst Parts of the Type

- Detached or absent-minded in daily affairs
- Prone to overthinking and procrastination
- Struggle with emotional expression or social nuance
- Can appear condescending or indifferent unintentionally
- Lose motivation when tasks become routine
- Under stress, withdraw completely into thought or fantasy

Growth and Development

INTPs grow by connecting ideas to action. Their mental agility becomes wisdom when paired with follow-through. Developing their inferior Extraverted Feeling helps them express care more openly and build stronger relationships.

They benefit from committing to practical goals—even small ones—to bridge theory and reality. When they learn that structure enhances creativity rather than restricts it, their potential expands dramatically.

At full maturity, INTPs become the true architects of insight: disciplined thinkers who can both design elegant systems and translate them into reality, uniting reason and imagination in equal measure.

INTP Compatibility

Friendship

High: INFP, INTJ, ENTP
Moderate: INTP, ISTP, ENFP, INFJ
Challenging: ESFJ, ESTJ, ESFP, ENFJ, ISTJ, ISFJ

Romantic

High: ENTP, INTJ, INFP
Moderate: INTP, INFJ
Challenging: ESFJ, ESTJ, ESFP, ENFJ, ISTJ, ISFJ, ENFP, ISTP

ESTP – The Dynamo

Core Traits

The ESTP personality type—*Extraverted, Sensing, Thinking, Perceiving*—is energetic, adaptable, and bold. Known as "The Dynamo" or "The Entrepreneur," ESTPs live for action. They thrive on momentum, challenge, and direct experience. Where others hesitate, they dive in. Where others plan, they improvise.

They are practical realists who trust their senses more than theories. Their attention is always tuned to the present moment—reading body language, spotting opportunity, and reacting faster than most people can think. To the ESTP, life is a hands-on experiment; they learn by doing, not by talking about it.

They value independence, competition, and effectiveness. They love to win, but even more than victory, they crave *engagement*. When fully absorbed in the moment, they feel alive.

Cognitive Overview

- **Dominant:** Extraverted Sensing (Se) – focuses sharply on the present and reacts with precision to real-world stimuli.
- **Auxiliary:** Introverted Thinking (Ti) – seeks internal logical consistency and accuracy in decisions.
- **Tertiary:** Extraverted Feeling (Fe) – reads social dynamics and builds rapport with others.
- **Inferior:** Introverted Intuition (Ni) – provides long-term insight and foresight, but develops later in life.

This function stack makes ESTPs dynamic and grounded. They balance real-time action with quick logic, adjusting seamlessly to shifting circumstances. They don't theorize about life—they *live* it.

Temperament as a Child

ESTP children are lively, curious, and daring. They prefer physical play to quiet study and often test boundaries just to see where they lie. They love competition, games, and exploration—especially activities with immediate rewards.

They are sharp observers of people and environments. If told something "can't be done," they will try anyway, partly to learn, partly to prove it wrong.

They need parents and teachers who channel their energy constructively rather than suppress it. Clear, consistent consequences work better than lectures or abstract reasoning. If guided wisely, their boldness becomes confidence rather than recklessness.

Temperament as an Adult

As adults, ESTPs are decisive and persuasive. They exude charisma and confidence, often becoming natural leaders in fast-moving environments. They enjoy challenges that test both their skill and adaptability—whether in business, sports, or negotiation.

They are pragmatic problem-solvers who cut through red tape to get results. However, they dislike long explanations and theoretical debates. For them, usefulness outweighs speculation.

Under stress, they can become impatient or thrill-seeking, chasing stimulation to avoid boredom. Maturity teaches them the value of reflection and restraint, allowing their insight (Ni) to balance their impulsiveness.

Best Learning Style

ESTPs learn best through **action and feedback**. They want to see immediate results and test knowledge in the real world. Lectures and abstract theory bore them; simulations, labs, and competitions excite them.

They thrive when allowed to experiment and move. They retain information when it's tied to practical application—show them how something works, and they'll master it faster than most.

They do best under teachers or mentors who challenge them, respect their autonomy, and keep lessons concrete and engaging.

Workplace Habits

In professional settings, ESTPs are confident, assertive, and results-driven. They thrive under pressure and are skilled at thinking on their feet. They excel in crisis management, negotiation, sales, emergency response, or entrepreneurship—anywhere decisiveness and adaptability matter.

They dislike excessive rules or drawn-out procedures. Efficiency, freedom, and tangible progress motivate them far more than hierarchy or routine.

Colleagues often admire their energy but may struggle with their bluntness. ESTPs value direct communication and have little patience for emotional subtext or hidden agendas.

Friendships

ESTPs are lively, loyal, and generous friends. They bring excitement to every group and can turn even mundane situations into memorable experiences. They are spontaneous planners—the ones who call at midnight with a great idea and expect you to say yes.

They enjoy physical or social activity with friends—sports, travel, projects, or competition. They are quick to defend those they care about, but they expect loyalty and honesty in return.

They dislike passive-aggressiveness or brooding. If there's an issue, they'd rather confront it head-on and move forward.

Love Life

In relationships, ESTPs are passionate, attentive, and straightforward. They love pursuit—the excitement of attraction, the thrill of spontaneity, and the adventure of discovery.

They show affection through action: planning trips, fixing problems, or simply being fully present. They appreciate partners who are confident, independent, and able to match their pace.

However, they can become restless in overly predictable relationships or feel trapped by too much emotional intensity. Their growth lies in recognizing that intimacy requires stillness as well as excitement. When mature, ESTPs become deeply loyal partners who balance passion with dependability.

Money Management

ESTPs are opportunistic with money—quick to spend, quick to earn, and confident in their ability to recover from setbacks. They often view money as a tool for freedom and fun rather than security.

They enjoy tangible rewards: travel, vehicles, hobbies, or technology. They are skilled negotiators and often excel at making money through fast-paced ventures or investments.

Their financial challenge is long-term planning. They prefer immediate gratification over delayed stability. Learning to budget and save strategically ensures their hard-won success lasts.

Best Parts of the Type

- Energetic, charismatic, and quick-thinking
- Fearless under pressure; thrive in crisis
- Excellent negotiators and real-time problem-solvers
- Adaptable and resourceful in any environment
- Naturally confident and persuasive communicators
- Bring excitement and momentum to projects and teams

Worst Parts of the Type

- Impulsive and risk-prone under boredom
- Struggle with long-term commitments or delayed gratification
- May overlook others' emotions or deeper needs
- Dislike rules and structure, leading to occasional chaos
- Can become manipulative or domineering when unchecked
- Under stress, may act recklessly or avoid reflection

Growth and Development

ESTPs grow by slowing down and reflecting on meaning rather than motion. Their instinct for action is powerful but can overshadow their long-term intuition (Ni). Developing patience and foresight helps them plan beyond the moment.

Cultivating empathy through their tertiary Extraverted Feeling allows them to balance boldness with sensitivity. When they learn that emotional intelligence strengthens influence, not weakens it, they become formidable leaders and companions.

At full maturity, ESTPs embody disciplined energy: decisive, adaptable, and wise—masters of both movement and mindfulness.

ESTP Compatibility

Friendship

High: ESFP, ISTP, ESTP
Moderate: ENTP, ESTJ, ISFP, ESFJ
Challenging: INFJ, INFP, INTJ, ENFJ, ISFJ, ISTJ

Romantic

High: ESFP, ISTP, ESTP
Moderate: ENTP, ISFP
Challenging: INFJ, INFP, INTJ, ENFJ, ESFJ, ESTJ, ISTJ

ESFP – The Performer

Core Traits

The ESFP personality type—*Extraverted, Sensing, Feeling, Perceiving*—is lively, warm, and expressive. Often called "The Performer" or "The Entertainer," ESFPs live in vivid color. They are the storytellers, improvisers, and empathic connectors who make life feel brighter.

They thrive on experience and human connection. Every moment is an opportunity for joy, movement, and meaning. They are acutely aware of their surroundings and draw energy from engaging with people and their environment.

Beneath their playfulness lies genuine sensitivity. ESFPs read emotional nuance instinctively and respond with warmth and authenticity. They are not performers for attention's sake—they perform to connect, uplift, and remind others that life can be beautiful right now.

Cognitive Overview

- **Dominant:** Extraverted Sensing (Se) – engages the world through direct experience and sensory detail.
- **Auxiliary:** Introverted Feeling (Fi) – makes decisions based on personal values and emotional authenticity.
- **Tertiary:** Extraverted Thinking (Te) – organizes and acts decisively when motivated by practical goals.
- **Inferior:** Introverted Intuition (Ni) – provides flashes of insight into long-term patterns but may feel abstract or overwhelming.

This combination produces a personality that is spontaneous but sincere, playful but grounded in empathy. ESFPs may seem carefree, but their emotions run deep and genuine.

Temperament as a Child

ESFP children are spirited, affectionate, and imaginative. They love sensory play—music, art, dancing, or exploring outdoors. They often become the heart of a group, effortlessly making friends and lifting others' moods.

They dislike rigidity or isolation and learn best through active participation. Punishment or excessive structure stifles them; encouragement and experiential learning make them shine.

They may struggle with delayed gratification and need gentle reminders to think beyond the moment. Parents who celebrate their enthusiasm while teaching patience help them mature into confident, kind adults.

Temperament as an Adult

As adults, ESFPs bring vibrancy to everything they touch. They are enthusiastic communicators who inspire teamwork and camaraderie. Their optimism, humor, and compassion make them magnetic in both friendships and professional settings.

They prefer experience to theory, action to abstraction. They are drawn to roles involving performance, teaching, counseling, hospitality, or healthcare—anywhere they can interact and bring comfort or joy to others.

When stressed, they can become restless, avoidant, or overwhelmed by emotion. Quiet reflection or creative outlets help them regain balance.

Best Learning Style

ESFPs learn best through **experiential and social engagement**. They need to touch, move, and experience what they're learning. They remember details vividly when tied to emotion or action.

They excel in collaborative, hands-on environments—fieldwork, labs, workshops, or group projects. They struggle with long theoretical lectures or repetitive tasks that lack human meaning.

Encouragement, recognition, and practical feedback motivate them more than strict evaluation.

Workplace Habits

At work, ESFPs are adaptable, cheerful, and people-centered. They bring emotional intelligence and enthusiasm to teams, often acting as mediators or morale boosters. They keep environments grounded, human, and lively.

They prefer fast-paced settings with visible results. Bureaucracy, abstract policy, or detached leadership frustrate them. Their best work happens when creativity and social connection are part of the process.

They shine in roles such as teaching, sales, healthcare, design, event planning, or performing arts. Their ability to connect makes them invaluable in any career requiring empathy and responsiveness.

Friendships

ESFPs are warm, loyal, and generous friends. They thrive on shared experiences—concerts, adventures, or spontaneous gatherings. They bring humor and empathy to every relationship, knowing intuitively how to make others feel seen and valued.

They dislike tension and often act as peacemakers. However, their friendliness can sometimes be mistaken for superficiality; in truth, they value genuine bonds deeply.

When hurt, they may withdraw quietly, preferring to process emotions alone rather than confront conflict head-on. Friends who offer steady understanding rather than criticism earn their lasting loyalty.

Love Life

In love, ESFPs are affectionate, spontaneous, and deeply devoted when their feelings are genuine. They express affection through touch, humor, and shared adventure. To them, love should be both comfortable and exciting.

They fall in love through experience—seeing how a partner behaves under real circumstances, not through promises or ideals. They value sincerity and emotional honesty above all.

They may struggle with long-term planning or routine, preferring to live moment to moment. Partners who combine stability with playfulness help them feel safe without feeling confined.

Money Management

ESFPs tend to treat money as a means for living, not hoarding. They spend freely on experiences, gifts, and enjoyment but dislike the feeling of financial insecurity. They can be surprisingly resourceful when motivated, especially when their independence is at stake.

They benefit from practical financial systems that limit impulsive spending without dampening spontaneity—automatic savings, short-term goals, or budgeting tied to personal reward.

When mature, they learn to balance pleasure with prudence, turning financial discipline into another form of self-expression and freedom.

Best Parts of the Type

- Warm, generous, and emotionally intelligent
- Charismatic and socially adaptable in any setting
- Natural entertainers who make others feel valued
- Grounded, realistic, and responsive under pressure
- Empathetic listeners and supportive friends
- Bring beauty, laughter, and life wherever they go

Worst Parts of the Type

- Impulsive and prone to overindulgence
- Avoid long-term planning or serious reflection
- Struggle with follow-through on commitments
- May take criticism personally or react defensively
- Can lose focus when excitement fades
- Under stress, may withdraw or overcompensate with activity

Growth and Development

ESFPs grow by slowing down and looking inward. Their natural ability to seize the moment is powerful, but growth requires perspective—understanding not just *what feels good now* but *what will matter later.*

Developing their inferior Introverted Intuition (Ni) helps them think strategically, while strengthening their tertiary Extraverted Thinking (Te) improves consistency and accountability.

When balanced, ESFPs evolve into wise optimists: still joyful and expressive, but now steady and self-aware—proof that passion and maturity can coexist.

ESFP Compatibility

Friendship

High: ISFP, ESTP, ESFP
Moderate: ESFJ, ENFP, ISTP, ENTP
Challenging: INTJ, INFJ, ESTJ, ENTJ, ISTJ, INTP

Romantic

High: ISFP, ESTP, ESFP
Moderate: ENFP, ESFJ
Challenging: INTJ, INFJ, ESTJ, ENTJ, ISTJ, ISTP, INTP, ENTP

ENFP – The Champion

Core Traits

The ENFP personality type—*Extraverted, Intuitive, Feeling, Perceiving*—is enthusiastic, imaginative, and idealistic. Known as "The Champion" or "The Campaigner," ENFPs radiate energy and optimism. They see potential in everyone and everything, often acting as catalysts for inspiration, creativity, and change.

Their minds are constantly alive with possibilities. They connect ideas, people, and causes through intuition and passion. They are natural encouragers—drawn to authenticity, personal growth, and the thrill of what could be.

Though playful and spontaneous, ENFPs take their values seriously. They are guided by inner conviction and empathy rather than convention or authority. They live to explore meaning and connection and to help others do the same.

Cognitive Overview

- **Dominant:** Extraverted Intuition (Ne) – explores connections, patterns, and potential outcomes in the external world.
- **Auxiliary:** Introverted Feeling (Fi) – anchors them in personal values and emotional authenticity.
- **Tertiary:** Extraverted Thinking (Te) – provides structure and execution when inspired.
- **Inferior:** Introverted Sensing (Si) – recalls experience and detail but may feel restrictive or easily ignored.

This function stack makes ENFPs visionaries of possibility—restless, creative, and compassionate. They are emotional idealists who can rally others toward shared purpose while maintaining independence of thought.

Temperament as a Child

ENFP children are lively, curious, and expressive. They see the world as a playground for ideas, stories, and discoveries. They ask endless questions—not to challenge, but to understand.

They are imaginative storytellers and compassionate friends, sensitive to fairness and emotional undercurrents. They need room to explore freely but benefit from gentle boundaries that teach focus and follow-through.

When criticized or stifled, they may retreat into fantasy or rebellion. Encouragement that validates their creativity while reinforcing responsibility helps them thrive.

Temperament as an Adult

As adults, ENFPs are vibrant, charismatic, and deeply empathetic. They excel at communication and often become the emotional heartbeat of their workplaces or communities. They bring enthusiasm to new ventures and inspire others with their contagious belief in human potential.

They prefer meaning over materialism, adventure over routine. Their energy fuels big ideas, but without discipline they can scatter their focus across too many projects. Learning to channel imagination through structure transforms their passion into achievement.

When stressed, ENFPs may feel trapped or disillusioned. They regain balance through solitude, journaling, or creative outlets that reconnect them to purpose.

Best Learning Style

ENFPs learn best through exploration and discussion. They absorb information through patterns, analogies, and emotional context rather than rote facts. They thrive when learning is interactive, imaginative, and infused with meaning.

They remember what *inspires* them, not what simply informs them. They benefit from mentors who allow curiosity, encourage personal interpretation, and provide variety and intellectual freedom.

Rigid, repetitive instruction drains them; open-ended challenges invigorate them.

Workplace Habits

In professional settings, ENFPs are creative, persuasive, and people-oriented. They motivate teams through enthusiasm and vision. They excel in roles requiring innovation, empathy, and communication—such as marketing, teaching, counseling, writing, or public relations.

They prefer flexible structures and meaningful projects. Bureaucratic rigidity frustrates them, while collaboration and purpose energize them. They are idea-generators who see connections others overlook.

Their weakness lies in follow-through; they may start passionately but lose interest when routine sets in. Support from organized colleagues or practical systems keeps them grounded.

Friendships

ENFPs are warm, expressive, and loyal friends who crave emotional depth and authenticity. They connect easily with people of all kinds and can make anyone feel understood.

They are generous with time and attention, remembering details that make others feel special. They prefer friendships built on honesty and shared growth rather than convenience.

When hurt, ENFPs may withdraw or overanalyze, oscillating between idealism and disillusionment. Honest communication and reassurance restore trust quickly.

They bring humor, empathy, and a sense of adventure to every friendship—turning ordinary moments into stories worth remembering.

Love Life

In love, ENFPs are romantic idealists who see relationships as journeys of mutual discovery. They seek a deep, soulful connection that feels both exciting and authentic.

They express affection through enthusiasm, curiosity, and imagination—planning surprises, offering insight, or simply making life more colorful. They value emotional honesty and intellectual chemistry equally.

They may idealize partners early on, seeing potential rather than reality. When expectations collide with imperfection, they must learn that real love thrives not in fantasy but in acceptance.

When emotionally secure, ENFPs are affectionate, devoted, and endlessly supportive. Their loyalty is grounded in shared vision, not obligation.

Money Management

ENFPs view money as freedom—the ability to explore, create, and give. They are often generous to a fault and may spend impulsively on experiences, causes, or loved ones.

They dislike financial restrictions and often postpone planning until necessary. Budgeting can feel creatively suffocating unless reframed as enabling independence.

They benefit from systems that are flexible but consistent—automatic savings, short-term goals, and accountability partners who understand their aversion to rigidity.

When mature, they balance passion with practicality, turning money into a means of sustaining meaning rather than chasing it.

Best Parts of the Type

- Enthusiastic, inspiring, and contagiously optimistic
- Empathetic and deeply attuned to others' emotions
- Creative, curious, and open to new experiences
- Skilled communicators who motivate and connect
- Values authenticity and emotional truth
- Capable of deep love, loyalty, and moral conviction

Worst Parts of the Type

- Easily distracted or overwhelmed by too many interests
- May idealize people or causes unrealistically
- Struggle with follow-through and consistency
- Sensitive to criticism and prone to burnout
- Can avoid conflict until resentment builds
- Under stress, may become disorganized or emotionally volatile

Growth and Development

ENFPs grow through focus and follow-through. Their gift for inspiration becomes power when grounded in discipline. Developing their tertiary Extraverted Thinking (Te) helps them organize ideas into sustainable action, while their inferior Introverted Sensing (Si) teaches patience and respect for experience.

They also grow by embracing rest and reflection; their constant mental motion can obscure self-awareness. When they learn to slow down, listen inwardly, and commit fully, they transform their creativity into lasting influence.

At full maturity, ENFPs embody radiant authenticity—hopeful visionaries who remind others that joy, kindness, and courage are revolutionary acts.

ENFP Compatibility

Friendship

High: INFJ, INTJ, ENTP
Moderate: ENFP, ENFJ, INFP, ISFP
Challenging: ESTJ, ISTJ, ESTP, ESFP, ISTP, ESFJ

Romantic

High: INFJ, INTJ, ENTP
Moderate: ENFP, INFP
Challenging: ESTJ, ISTJ, ESTP, ESFP, ISTP, ENTJ, ESFJ, ENFJ

ENTP – The Visionary

Core Traits

The ENTP personality type—*Extraverted, Intuitive, Thinking, Perceiving*—is inventive, energetic, and intellectually restless. Known as "The Visionary" or "The Debater," ENTPs are masters of innovation and argumentation. They delight in ideas that challenge assumptions, and they often play devil's advocate not to provoke, but to expand perspective.

They thrive on possibility and complexity. Where others see problems, ENTPs see potential. Their quick wit and mental agility allow them to navigate unfamiliar topics effortlessly, finding connections that others overlook. They are the entrepreneurs, inventors, and thinkers who push boundaries simply because stagnation feels like death.

Freedom of thought and flexibility of approach define them. For an ENTP, curiosity is not a trait—it's a way of life.

Cognitive Overview

- **Dominant:** Extraverted Intuition (Ne) – generates ideas, explores patterns, and finds possibilities everywhere.
- **Auxiliary:** Introverted Thinking (Ti) – tests ideas logically and seeks internal coherence.
- **Tertiary:** Extraverted Feeling (Fe) – connects socially and reads emotional dynamics.
- **Inferior:** Introverted Sensing (Si) – recalls precedent and detail, often ignored until stress demands structure.

This cognitive structure produces a mind that is daring, fast, and endlessly inventive. ENTPs juggle ideas like acrobats, experimenting constantly with new angles and concepts.

Temperament as a Child

ENTP children are imaginative, talkative, and endlessly inquisitive. They are the ones constantly asking "why?"—not to be difficult, but because the world fascinates them.

They enjoy mental challenges and thrive when encouraged to explore, build, and experiment. They resist rigid authority and may challenge teachers or parents who can't justify rules logically.

They learn best when allowed to question, debate, and test ideas through direct experience. Adults who respond with patience and respect help shape their curiosity into brilliance rather than rebellion.

Temperament as an Adult

As adults, ENTPs become dynamic thinkers and energetic innovators. They love variety and intellectual stimulation and grow restless when confined to routine. They thrive in situations that demand problem-solving, quick thinking, and adaptability.

They are charming conversationalists—persuasive, humorous, and fearless in debate. They enjoy exploring unconventional ideas and can shift perspectives effortlessly. However, their enthusiasm sometimes outpaces practicality, leading to abandoned projects or scattered energy.

At their best, they are visionary leaders; at their worst, they are brilliant procrastinators.

Best Learning Style

ENTPs learn through exploration, dialogue, and experimentation. They need intellectual stimulation and freedom to question. Abstract theory excites them when it connects to real-world potential.

They absorb information rapidly and prefer conceptual discussion over rote memorization. Group debates, open-ended projects, and brainstorming sessions suit them perfectly.

Repetition bores them; discovery energizes them. Teachers who engage their curiosity and allow intellectual autonomy bring out their full brilliance.

Workplace Habits

In professional life, ENTPs are inventive, adaptable, and bold. They excel in dynamic fields—entrepreneurship, marketing, law, consulting, technology, media—where creativity and agility are prized.

They are natural idea generators, often serving as catalysts for innovation. They challenge inefficiency and reimagine systems. However, their enthusiasm for new ventures can make them impatient with maintenance or follow-up.

They prefer freedom to experiment and dislike micromanagement. Teams value their creativity but may need to help implement their flood of ideas.

ENTPs lead best through vision and persuasion rather than control. They motivate others by showing possibilities, not by enforcing rules.

Friendships

ENTPs are stimulating and charismatic friends who thrive on intellectual connection. They enjoy witty banter, late-night debates, and shared adventures. They surround themselves with people who can match their mental pace or challenge their assumptions.

They are playful and open-minded, capable of talking to anyone about anything. They prefer honesty—even bluntness—to tactful vagueness.

While loyal to those who understand their need for independence, they may drift away from friendships that feel stagnant or overly emotional. Their affection is shown through engagement—if an ENTP debates you, it means they value you.

Love Life

In relationships, ENTPs are passionate, curious, and unpredictable. They seek partners who are intellectually stimulating, confident, and open to growth. They are drawn to mental chemistry as much as emotional connection.

They show affection through attention, humor, and creative expression. Routine bores them; they prefer relationships that evolve and challenge both partners to grow.

Their challenge lies in consistency—they may chase novelty or avoid emotional depth when it feels restrictive. With maturity, they learn that stability and adventure can coexist.

When grounded, ENTPs are loyal, spontaneous, and deeply invested in shared discovery.

Money Management

ENTPs view money as a resource for exploration and experimentation. They enjoy taking calculated risks—investments, startups, or new ventures—especially if they promise intellectual or creative payoff.

They are often financially successful due to resourcefulness and persuasion but can lose focus on budgeting or long-term savings. They dislike routine accounting and may procrastinate on financial details.

Their growth comes from learning to view financial structure as a launchpad for freedom, not a constraint on it. When they discipline their creativity, they often achieve remarkable prosperity.

Best Parts of the Type

- Brilliant innovators who thrive on complexity and change
- Charismatic communicators with humor and insight
- Fearless thinkers who question convention and spark progress
- Naturally persuasive and adaptable in any situation
- Enthusiastic, optimistic, and intellectually generous
- Capable of great vision and originality when inspired

Worst Parts of the Type

- Easily distracted by new ideas; struggle to finish projects
- May argue for sport, alienating sensitive people
- Dislike structure and authority, risking disorganization
- Can appear arrogant or dismissive of emotion
- Under stress, may overanalyze or become scattered
- Tend to prioritize novelty over stability

Growth and Development

ENTPs grow by cultivating discipline and empathy. Their mental speed and inventiveness can scatter their energy without structure. Developing their tertiary Extraverted Feeling (Fe) allows them to connect more deeply and use charm responsibly.

Their inferior Introverted Sensing (Si) teaches patience and respect for experience. When they learn to balance creativity with continuity, they become true innovators—both dreamers and builders.

At full maturity, ENTPs embody visionary pragmatism: audacious enough to imagine what's next, wise enough to see it through, and generous enough to bring others along for the ride.

ENTP Compatibility

Friendship

High: ENFP, INFJ, INTP
Moderate: ENTP, ENFJ, INTJ, ESTP
Challenging: ISFJ, ESFJ, ISTJ, ESTJ, ISFP, ESFP

Romantic

High: INFJ, ENFP, INTP
Moderate: ENTP, INTJ
Challenging: ISFJ, ESFJ, ISTJ, ESTJ, ISFP, ESFP, ENFJ, ESTP

ESTJ – The Supervisor

Core Traits

The ESTJ personality type—*Extraverted, Sensing, Thinking, Judging*—is organized, decisive, and duty-driven. Known as "The Supervisor" or "The Executive," ESTJs are the backbone of structure and order. They believe that systems work best when rules are clear, responsibilities are honored, and effort is measurable.

They are practical leaders who value tradition, accountability, and competence. When others hesitate, ESTJs take charge, setting goals, clarifying expectations, and ensuring that standards are met. Their world operates on logic and reliability—two things they bring to every project, relationship, and organization.

ESTJs don't seek chaos or novelty; they seek results. They are the ones who turn ideals into action and ideas into reality.

Cognitive Overview

- **Dominant:** Extraverted Thinking (Te) – organizes and executes efficiently using logic and structure.
- **Auxiliary:** Introverted Sensing (Si) – recalls past experience to ensure stability and consistency.
- **Tertiary:** Extraverted Intuition (Ne) – explores new ideas when grounded in practicality.
- **Inferior:** Introverted Feeling (Fi) – provides quiet personal values that may be hard to express outwardly.

This function stack gives ESTJs a commanding presence. They are pragmatic, focused, and confident in decision-making, preferring clarity over ambiguity and proof over theory.

Temperament as a Child

ESTJ children are assertive, responsible, and self-directed. They often take on leadership roles naturally, organizing games, enforcing rules, and ensuring fairness (as they define it).

They enjoy structure and predictability, preferring routines that make sense. They can be outspoken and stubborn, especially when rules feel inconsistent or illogical.

They thrive under parents and teachers who provide clear boundaries and respect their independence. Praise for diligence and dependability encourages them to lead responsibly rather than rigidly.

Temperament as an Adult

As adults, ESTJs are confident managers of people and processes. They excel in environments where order, logic, and accountability drive success. They are often found in administrative, leadership, or managerial roles—positions that require decisiveness and dependability.

They are direct communicators who value efficiency and action. They tend to focus on measurable progress rather than abstract ideals. However, they are not without emotion; their loyalty runs deep, even if their affection is shown through responsibility more than sentiment.

When stressed, ESTJs may become inflexible or overly critical, believing that if others simply "did things right," problems would disappear. Balance comes when they recognize that empathy and patience can enhance, not hinder, efficiency.

Best Learning Style

ESTJs learn best through **structured, practical methods**. They value clear goals, concrete examples, and logical explanations. They prefer material that has real-world relevance and can be applied immediately.

They are detail-oriented and thrive in systems that reward preparation and discipline. They dislike vague discussions or speculative theory unless tied to a tangible outcome.

They excel in learning environments with defined expectations, measurable progress, and authority figures they respect.

Workplace Habits

In the workplace, ESTJs are natural organizers and enforcers of standards. They excel in roles that demand structure—operations, management, law enforcement, business administration, military service, and logistics.

They approach work methodically, ensuring that resources are used efficiently and objectives are achieved. They set high standards for themselves and others, often becoming the "anchor" of their teams.

While respected for their leadership, they may struggle to adapt to rapidly changing circumstances or tolerate ambiguity. They function best in stable systems that reward consistency and clear results.

Their ideal work environment values competence, responsibility, and teamwork—and wastes no time on empty talk.

Friendships

ESTJs are dependable and loyal friends who show care through action rather than words. They're the ones who organize gatherings, remember commitments, and ensure things get done.

They prefer friendships grounded in shared values, mutual respect, and reliability. They are protective of those they care about and will defend friends with unwavering loyalty.

However, they may come across as overly blunt or controlling if they believe someone is acting irresponsibly. Learning to listen before advising strengthens their relationships.

For ESTJs, friendship is a matter of trust and consistency. They value people who mean what they say and follow through.

Love Life

In love, ESTJs are steadfast, responsible partners who approach relationships with the same commitment they bring to their work. They express affection through dependability, practical support, and shared goals rather than through overt romantic gestures.

They are attracted to partners who are grounded, loyal, and capable of mutual respect. They dislike games or emotional unpredictability; honesty and stability matter more than sentimentality.

Conflict rarely frightens them—they prefer to address problems directly and logically. However, they can unintentionally come across as dismissive of emotions if they overvalue reason.

When balanced, ESTJs make devoted, trustworthy, and lifelong partners who turn promises into practice.

Money Management

ESTJs are generally excellent with money. They value financial security, planning, and long-term stability. They prefer predictable systems—budgets, savings plans, and investments grounded in logic rather than speculation.

They dislike debt and financial chaos, viewing them as signs of poor discipline. They are often early planners for retirement, property, and family security.

Their challenge lies in balancing pragmatism with enjoyment; they may be so focused on stability that they forget to relax or indulge occasionally. When mature, they learn that financial health is not just about control, but about balance.

Best Parts of the Type

- Highly organized, reliable, and decisive
- Strong leaders who uphold order and standards
- Excellent at execution and logistical planning
- Loyal and consistent in relationships and commitments
- Courageous in crisis; calm under pressure
- Committed to fairness, duty, and community responsibility

Worst Parts of the Type

- Can be rigid or controlling under stress
- Struggle with emotional expression or empathy
- Dislike ambiguity and resist untested ideas
- May judge others too quickly or harshly
- Overwork themselves, neglecting rest or creativity
- Under pressure, may equate authority with moral correctness

Growth and Development

ESTJs grow by learning to temper control with compassion. Their leadership becomes transformative when they value flexibility as much as efficiency. Developing their inferior Introverted Feeling (Fi) helps them connect to personal values and understand emotional nuance.

They also grow by listening before deciding—recognizing that diverse perspectives can strengthen rather than weaken structure.

At full maturity, ESTJs become wise stewards of stability: disciplined but empathetic, structured but adaptable, and respected not only for what they achieve, but for the integrity with which they lead.

ESTJ Compatibility

Friendship

High: ISFJ, ESFJ, ISTJ
Moderate: ESTJ, ESTP, ENTJ, ISTP
Challenging: INFP, ENFP, INFJ, ENFJ, ESFP, ENTP, INTJ

Romantic

High: ISFJ, ESFJ, ISTJ
Moderate: ESTJ, INTJ
Challenging: INFP, ENFP, INFJ, ENFJ, ESFP, ISTP, ENTP, ENTJ

ESFJ – The Provider

Core Traits

The ESFJ personality type—*Extraverted, Sensing, Feeling, Judging*—is warm, dependable, and community-minded. Known as "The Provider" or "The Caregiver," ESFJs thrive on creating harmony and stability for the people around them. They are the glue that holds groups together—organizing, nurturing, and ensuring that everyone feels included and cared for.

They are deeply attuned to others' emotions and social needs. Where some types focus on abstract ideas, ESFJs focus on people—their comfort, their happiness, their well-being. They value duty, tradition, and kindness, believing that a good life is built on responsibility and connection.

At their core, ESFJs want life to make sense *socially*—for everyone to know their place, feel appreciated, and contribute meaningfully to the whole.

Cognitive Overview

- **Dominant:** Extraverted Feeling (Fe) – reads emotional cues and maintains social harmony.
- **Auxiliary:** Introverted Sensing (Si) – recalls personal experience and traditions for stability.
- **Tertiary:** Extraverted Intuition (Ne) – recognizes patterns and new possibilities in relationships.
- **Inferior:** Introverted Thinking (Ti) – seeks internal logic but may feel uncomfortable relying on it.

This combination produces a personality that is empathetic yet pragmatic—someone who values both emotional connection and tangible results. ESFJs are caretakers by instinct and organizers by skill.

Temperament as a Child

ESFJ children are affectionate, cooperative, and eager to please. They crave approval from parents and teachers and are happiest when they know they are helping. They enjoy order, teamwork, and predictable routines, often taking on responsibilities early.

They are sensitive to tone and criticism—what feels like mild disapproval to others can feel like rejection to them. Encouragement and appreciation motivate them far more effectively than punishment.

They thrive in warm, structured environments that reinforce fairness, compassion, and reliability.

Temperament as an Adult

As adults, ESFJs become pillars of dependability. They are often found at the center of families, offices, or communities, ensuring that needs are met and things run smoothly. They take genuine pleasure in caring for others and maintaining harmony.

They value loyalty, manners, and responsibility, and they tend to judge character by consistency of behavior. They are traditionalists in spirit—trusting systems that have proven their worth.

When stressed or unappreciated, they can become controlling or overly self-sacrificing, believing that others don't notice their efforts. Balance comes when they recognize that self-care is not selfish but essential.

Best Learning Style

ESFJs learn best in **structured, relational environments**. They prefer material with practical value and real-world application. Clear expectations, step-by-step instruction, and supportive feedback help them thrive.

They remember through repetition and personal association—connecting facts to people or experiences. They enjoy cooperative learning and prefer teachers who are personable, clear, and organized.

Abstract theory without context can frustrate them, but once they see *why* it matters, their work ethic and memory make them excellent students.

Workplace Habits

In the workplace, ESFJs are responsible, loyal, and detail-oriented. They excel in roles that require empathy, organization, and direct service—such as teaching, healthcare, administration, hospitality, or human resources.

They are diligent team players who value harmony and follow established systems faithfully. They often rise to leadership because others trust their reliability and fairness.

Their challenge lies in overextending themselves to meet others' needs or becoming anxious when systems change unexpectedly. They prefer stable, cooperative work cultures with clear hierarchies and mutual respect.

Friendships

ESFJs are generous, thoughtful friends who take pleasure in supporting and celebrating others. They remember birthdays, lend practical help, and create gatherings where everyone feels welcome.

They value closeness and shared experiences. Friendship, to them, is a promise of mutual care and loyalty. They dislike distance or coldness and may worry excessively if they sense tension.

They must occasionally step back to ensure they're not giving more than they receive. Their empathy is deep, but balance keeps it healthy.

Love Life

In relationships, ESFJs are devoted and affectionate. They express love through consistent attention, acts of service, and emotional availability. They want harmony and stability—and will work tirelessly to preserve both.

They are attracted to partners who appreciate reliability and communication. They dislike emotional games and prefer clear, honest affection.

They sometimes take on too much responsibility for a partner's happiness, equating love with caretaking. When they learn that love also includes self-expression and boundaries, they flourish.

At their best, ESFJs make loving, dependable partners who turn affection into daily devotion.

Money Management

ESFJs are careful and conscientious with money. They value security and tend to budget responsibly, often prioritizing family and community needs above personal luxury.

They prefer predictable systems—steady income, savings accounts, and concrete plans. They dislike financial risk and uncertainty.

Their generosity, however, can lead to overspending on others. They feel most at peace when finances are both stable and meaningful—used to nurture relationships or create comfort for loved ones.

Best Parts of the Type

- Compassionate, loyal, and attentive to others' needs
- Highly organized and dependable
- Skilled communicators who create harmony
- Generous and emotionally intelligent
- Practical, hardworking, and trustworthy
- Maintain traditions and strengthen communities

Worst Parts of the Type

- Can become overbearing or controlling under stress
- Overly sensitive to criticism or perceived rejection
- May neglect personal needs for others' comfort
- Struggle with abstract or rapidly changing environments
- Can equate moral worth with social approval
- Under pressure, may suppress individuality to avoid conflict

Growth and Development

ESFJs grow by valuing self-reflection as much as service. Their compassion becomes stronger when it includes themselves. Developing their inferior Introverted Thinking (Ti) helps them make balanced decisions and rely less on external validation.

They also grow by learning to tolerate uncertainty—recognizing that not all problems can be solved through order or consensus.

At full maturity, ESFJs become wise caretakers of community and conscience: still nurturing, still practical, but now balanced with insight and independence. They embody the best of warmth and wisdom—proof that kindness, when tempered with clarity, is one of humanity's greatest strengths.

ESFJ Compatibility

Friendship

High: ISFJ, ESFJ, ESTJ
Moderate: ESFP, ENFJ, ESTP, ISFP
Challenging: INTP, ISTP, INTJ, ENTP, ENFP, INFJ

Romantic

High: ISFJ, ESFJ, ESTJ
Moderate: ESFP, ENFJ
Challenging: INTP, ISTP, INTJ, ENTP, ENFP, INFJ, ESTP, ISFP

ENFJ – The Teacher

Core Traits

The ENFJ personality type—*Extraverted, Intuitive, Feeling, Judging*—is charismatic, empathetic, and purpose-driven. Known as "The Teacher" or "The Protagonist," ENFJs are natural leaders who uplift others through encouragement and vision. They see potential in people and feel a deep responsibility to help that potential flourish.

They are emotionally intelligent and socially adept, able to sense what others need almost before it's expressed. They lead with warmth and persuasion rather than authority, inspiring cooperation instead of demanding it. For ENFJs, leadership is not about power—it's about guidance, unity, and growth.

They thrive on meaning and connection, striving to make their relationships and communities better through understanding and shared purpose.

Cognitive Overview

- **Dominant:** Extraverted Feeling (Fe) – harmonizes social environments and responds to emotional needs.
- **Auxiliary:** Introverted Intuition (Ni) – envisions future possibilities and aligns actions with purpose.
- **Tertiary:** Extraverted Sensing (Se) – engages with the external world and appreciates sensory experiences.
- **Inferior:** Introverted Thinking (Ti) – provides logical precision, but can be underdeveloped or emotionally detached.

This combination makes ENFJs natural mentors—people who blend insight with empathy, persuasion with sincerity. They bring people together around shared ideals and are often the moral compass in their circles.

Temperament as a Child

ENFJ children are outgoing, expressive, and caring. They instinctively try to make others happy and may act as little diplomats in their families or classrooms. They are natural communicators who pick up emotional subtleties quickly, often sensing tension before anyone speaks.

They value praise and emotional harmony. Criticism can wound them deeply, but reassurance helps them recover quickly.

They thrive when trusted with responsibility and encouraged to express ideas and creativity. Over-scheduling or perfectionist pressure, however, can cause anxiety—they must learn that it's okay to say no.

Temperament as an Adult

As adults, ENFJs become confident, persuasive, and compassionate leaders. They gravitate toward professions involving people—education, counseling, public service, ministry, management, or diplomacy. They excel at motivating others and building consensus.

They are visionary but grounded, able to see both the ideal future (Ni) and the concrete steps (Fe + Se) needed to make it real. However, they can overextend themselves, taking on others' burdens until they burn out.

When healthy, they embody optimism, purpose, and grace. When stressed, they may become overbearing or controlling, mistaking guidance for obligation. Balance comes when they remember that every person's growth must be self-driven.

Best Learning Style

ENFJs learn best through **interactive, human-centered learning**. They retain information when it connects to personal meaning or social impact. They thrive on discussion, collaboration, and real-world application rather than detached analysis.

They appreciate teachers who are encouraging, organized, and expressive. They excel at interpreting emotional tone and group dynamics, often helping others grasp difficult material by reframing it empathetically.

Abstract or impersonal instruction can bore them unless tied to human behavior, motivation, or transformation.

Workplace Habits

In the workplace, ENFJs are organized, proactive, and inspirational. They motivate teams through encouragement and shared purpose. They lead by example, emphasizing communication and fairness.

They thrive in roles that allow them to help others grow—management, teaching, coaching, public relations, or humanitarian work. They dislike environments driven solely by profit or competition.

They work best when tasks feel meaningful and teamwork is valued. However, they can struggle to delegate or say no, often assuming too much responsibility for the well-being of colleagues.

For ENFJs, leadership isn't about control; it's about service.

Friendships

ENFJs are loyal, nurturing friends who invest deeply in their relationships. They're generous with time and affection, often remembering birthdays, small details, and private struggles that others forget.

They want to see their friends succeed and will offer advice, encouragement, or a listening ear without hesitation. Their empathy makes them confidants, but they must take care not to absorb others' emotions to their own detriment.

They prefer friendships built on honesty and emotional reciprocity. Few types give more genuinely—or expect less recognition in return.

Love Life

In love, ENFJs are expressive, devoted, and idealistic. They love wholeheartedly and want relationships that grow and evolve. They believe in partnership as a collaboration—two people becoming more through each other's presence.

They express affection through attention, verbal affirmation, and consistent effort. They anticipate their partner's needs and work tirelessly to maintain harmony.

Their greatest challenge is overgiving—placing a partner's happiness above their own. They must learn that healthy love allows both people to flourish independently.

At their best, ENFJs make romantic relationships deeply fulfilling—a blend of trust, passion, and shared vision.

Money Management

ENFJs are responsible with money but motivated more by values than numbers. They see finances as a way to provide stability and support causes or loved ones. They're generous givers, often contributing to charities, family needs, or personal development.

They prefer organization—budgets, plans, and clear goals—but may struggle with long-term restraint if emotional causes tug at their heart. They must balance generosity with sustainability.

When mature, ENFJs align financial planning with moral purpose, ensuring both security and meaning coexist.

Best Parts of the Type

- Charismatic and inspirational leaders
- Deeply empathetic and emotionally perceptive
- Organized and goal-oriented with strong values
- Skilled communicators and motivators
- Loyal and devoted in relationships
- Combine vision with practical compassion

Worst Parts of the Type

- Can become controlling or overprotective
- Struggle to separate others' needs from their own
- Sensitive to criticism or perceived failure
- May neglect self-care while serving others
- Overcommit and burn out easily
- Under stress, become rigid in enforcing ideals

Growth and Development

ENFJs grow by setting emotional boundaries and trusting others' autonomy. Their gift for guidance becomes more powerful when they allow space for others to learn through mistakes.

Developing their inferior Introverted Thinking (Ti) brings clarity and balance, helping them analyze objectively rather than react emotionally. It turns their intuition into wisdom rather than obligation.

They also benefit from cultivating rest—learning that being still and receptive is as important as being active and helpful.

At full maturity, ENFJs embody compassionate leadership: inspiring others not through authority, but through authenticity, insight, and love rooted in wisdom.

ENFJ Compatibility

Friendship

High: INFJ, ENFP, INFP
Moderate: ENFJ, ENTP, ESFJ, INTJ
Challenging: ISTJ, ESTJ, ESFP, ESTP, ISTP, ISFJ

Romantic

High: INFJ, INTJ, ENFP
Moderate: ENFJ, INFP
Challenging: ISTJ, ESTJ, ESFP, ESTP, ISTP, ISFJ, ENTP

ENTJ – The Commander

Core Traits

The ENTJ personality type—*Extraverted, Intuitive, Thinking, Judging*—is strategic, assertive, and visionary. Known as "The Commander" or "The Executive," ENTJs are natural leaders who thrive on challenge, structure, and achievement. They see inefficiency as an obstacle to progress and instinctively look for ways to organize people and systems toward a goal.

They are forward-thinking, confident, and unafraid of conflict. Where others hesitate, ENTJs take decisive action. They value competence, efficiency, and ambition—not for vanity's sake, but because progress requires clarity and discipline.

ENTJs think in long arcs. Their plans often extend years into the future, yet they can adapt quickly when strategy demands it. Beneath their commanding presence lies an analytical mind constantly scanning for opportunity.

Cognitive Overview

- **Dominant:** Extraverted Thinking (Te) – drives organization, structure, and logical decision-making.
- **Auxiliary:** Introverted Intuition (Ni) – identifies long-term patterns and underlying causes.
- **Tertiary:** Extraverted Sensing (Se) – engages directly with reality, staying alert and responsive.
- **Inferior:** Introverted Feeling (Fi) – houses personal values, often underdeveloped or private.

This combination produces a powerful leader—objective, focused, and visionary. ENTJs see the "big picture" and have the willpower to turn vision into reality.

Temperament as a Child

ENTJ children are independent, articulate, and competitive. They often assume leadership roles among peers, organizing activities or enforcing rules. They value fairness but define it logically rather than emotionally.

They dislike inefficiency and can become impatient when others fail to meet expectations. However, when guided with balance—encouraged to lead without dominating—they develop a strong sense of integrity and respect for others' strengths.

They thrive under parents and teachers who challenge them intellectually and reward initiative, rather than compliance.

Temperament as an Adult

As adults, ENTJs become dynamic strategists. They are drawn to environments where they can innovate, lead, and drive change—business, law, engineering, politics, or the military. They are decisive, direct, and confident in their ability to take charge.

They command respect through competence and vision rather than charm alone. They are ambitious but not impulsive; they prefer deliberate planning over chance.

When stressed, ENTJs can become domineering or dismissive, especially toward inefficiency or emotional arguments. Balance comes when they learn that not all value is quantifiable—and that empathy can strengthen leadership, not weaken it.

Best Learning Style

ENTJs learn best through **structured, goal-oriented challenge**. They prefer systems of knowledge they can master and apply to solve real problems. They enjoy competition, debate, and measurable progress.

They value instructors who are competent, organized, and direct. They are independent learners who respect authority only when it demonstrates expertise.

They excel in academic and professional settings that reward initiative, logic, and achievement.

Workplace Habits

In the workplace, ENTJs are natural executives—decisive, organized, and relentless in pursuit of efficiency. They are skilled at delegation and long-term planning and often rise quickly into leadership roles.

They thrive in structured yet dynamic environments—corporate management, strategic consulting, entrepreneurship, or public administration. They prefer objective metrics and clear hierarchies but are also innovators who welcome calculated risk.

They can appear intimidating or blunt, especially when under pressure. However, their focus on competence and progress earns them deep respect. For ENTJs, work is a proving ground—an arena for mastery.

Friendships

ENTJs are loyal and intellectually stimulating friends. They admire confidence, independence, and drive in others. Their friendships often revolve around shared goals, mutual respect, and lively debate.

They are generous with advice but can come across as instructive. They express care by helping others improve—whether through mentoring, organizing, or challenging them to grow.

They respect honesty over flattery and prefer friends who match their directness. Their ideal friendships are built on mutual challenge and shared ambition.

Love Life

In relationships, ENTJs are passionate, protective, and committed. They approach love as both an emotional connection and a partnership of equals. They seek a partner who is confident, intelligent, and capable of independent thought.

They express affection through loyalty, consistency, and tangible effort—planning for the future, solving problems, or providing stability. They are less inclined toward sentimental gestures, preferring practical devotion over poetic words.

Their challenge lies in balancing control with empathy. They may unintentionally dominate discussions or dismiss emotions they don't understand. When they learn to listen with the same intensity they lead, relationships become their greatest strength.

At their best, ENTJs make loyal, dependable partners who build lives—rather than merely share them.

Money Management

ENTJs are typically excellent with money. They see finances as a tool for progress and security, not indulgence. They set goals, track progress, and invest strategically. They are disciplined savers and confident investors.

They prefer measurable results—balance sheets, long-term plans, and strategic reinvestment. Waste frustrates them as much in money as in time.

Their risk lies in overconfidence or in neglecting emotional considerations in financial decisions. When mature, they balance ambition with ethical stewardship, turning success into stability for themselves and others.

Best Parts of the Type

- Decisive, strategic, and goal-oriented
- Strong, competent leaders with clear vision
- Fearless in challenge and efficient under pressure
- Logical, articulate, and persuasive communicators
- Loyal and protective toward loved ones
- Thrive on growth, innovation, and excellence

Worst Parts of the Type

- Can be domineering or impatient with inefficiency
- May overlook emotional nuance or empathy
- Intolerant of weakness or indecision
- Risk overworking themselves and others
- Struggle to relax or admit vulnerability
- Under stress, may become blunt, dismissive, or controlling

Growth and Development

ENTJs grow by learning to integrate emotion and humanity into their leadership. Their natural command becomes far more powerful when tempered by empathy and active listening.

Developing their inferior Introverted Feeling (Fi) helps them understand values and motivations beyond metrics. This emotional intelligence allows them to lead not just through direction, but through inspiration.

They also benefit from slowing down—recognizing that rest and reflection are strategic tools, not weaknesses.

At full maturity, ENTJs become visionary builders of both systems and people—decisive yet compassionate, ambitious yet ethical, capable of transforming not only organizations, but lives.

ENTJ Compatibility

Friendship

High: ENTP, INTJ, ENFP
Moderate: ENTJ, ISTJ, ENFJ, ISTP
Challenging: INFP, ISFP, ESFP, ESTP, ISFJ, ESFJ

Romantic

High: ENTP, INTJ, ENFP
Moderate: ENTJ, INFP
Challenging: ISFP, ESFP, ESTP, ISFJ, ESFJ, ISTJ, ISTP

Part II: Beyond Typology

Chapter 1: Personality vs. Personality Disorder

Introduction

Most people use the word *personality* to mean the visible surface of behavior: habits, humor, confidence, or charm. Psychology uses the term differently: personality is the internal system of patterns that make behavior consistent over time. It includes how we think, feel, and relate to others.

A *personality type* describes preferences within the normal range of human functioning. A *personality disorder*, by contrast, describes patterns that are rigid, persistent, and self-defeating. The difference is not a matter of good versus bad character; it's a matter of **flexibility and consequence**.

Healthy Personality

A healthy personality is adaptable. It allows you to change tone for different situations, to learn from mistakes, to balance your own needs with those of others. Your MBTI type, for example, points to your *default* style, where you naturally start, but healthy functioning means you can use other styles when circumstances demand. Flexibility is the sign of mental health.

Healthy personalities:

- recognize and correct their own errors;
- adjust behavior based on feedback;
- maintain empathy, even under stress;
- can tolerate uncertainty without falling apart.

In short, a healthy personality *serves* you; it doesn't imprison you.

Disordered Personality

A personality becomes *disordered* when the patterns that once helped a person survive begin to cause repeated harm, to themselves or to others, and the person cannot adapt. The key traits are **rigidity**, **distortion**, and **impairment**.

Someone with a personality disorder tends to interpret the world through one unchanging lens, even when that lens repeatedly produces conflict or pain. They may be convinced that everyone else is wrong, that feedback is attack, or that manipulation is survival. These are not preferences; they are entrenched defenses.

Clinical psychology recognizes ten primary personality disorders, grouped broadly into three "clusters":

- **Cluster A (Odd or Eccentric):** Paranoid, Schizoid, Schizotypal.
- **Cluster B (Dramatic or Erratic):** Antisocial, Borderline, Histrionic, Narcissistic.
- **Cluster C (Anxious or Fearful):** Avoidant, Dependent, Obsessive-Compulsive Personality Disorder.

The names sound harsh, but remember that these labels describe enduring *patterns*, not momentary moods. Only a qualified clinician can diagnose them after thorough evaluation.

The Spectrum of Functioning

Healthy and disordered personality exist on a **continuum**, not a switch. Everyone occasionally shows traits from the disordered side (defensiveness, perfectionism, or emotional volatility) especially under stress. That does not mean they "have" a disorder. Diagnosis depends on **persistence, severity, and impairment**: the degree to which behavior consistently damages relationships, work, or well-being.

Think of it like this:

- A *type* explains what feels natural.
- A *trait* explains what happens under pressure.
- A *disorder* explains what a person can't stop doing, even when it no longer works.

Why the Distinction Matters

Confusing typology with pathology leads to judgment and misuse. Calling someone a "narcissist" because they're confident, or "borderline" because they're emotional, distorts both compassion and accuracy. Typology helps us understand **style**; clinical psychology helps us understand **suffering**.

When you label normal difference as disorder, you insult diversity. When you treat real disorders as quirks, you dismiss pain. Knowing the difference allows empathy in both directions.

Reflection Exercise

Think of a recent conflict or frustration with someone. Ask yourself:

- Was the issue about *preference* (different communication styles)?
- Was it about *stress* (temporary defensiveness or fear)?
- Or was it about *rigidity* (the same destructive pattern repeating despite consequences)?

Your answer reveals whether you're seeing a difference in personality type, a situational reaction, or something deeper that may require professional help.

Summary

Typology and pathology are cousins, not twins. One helps you appreciate variation in normal human functioning; the other helps identify when personality becomes its own obstacle. Understanding both prevents misuse of labels and strengthens your ability to respond to others — not with condemnation, but with clarity.

Chapter 2: Narcissism: The Spectrum, Not the Buzzword

Introduction

Few psychological terms have been emptied of meaning faster than *narcissist*. Online, it has become shorthand for anyone selfish, rude, or disappointing. In clinical psychology, however, narcissism describes a specific pattern of self-esteem regulation; an unstable identity propped up by admiration. Understanding that distinction protects both accuracy and compassion.

What Narcissism Actually Is

At its core, narcissism involves a deep conflict between **grandiosity** and **fragility**. The person depends on external validation to feel worthwhile, yet reacts defensively when criticized. Their sense of self expands and collapses like a balloon: impressive when inflated, empty when punctured.

Psychologists describe narcissism as a **spectrum**.

- **Healthy narcissism** is ordinary self-respect — confidence, pride in accomplishment, willingness to lead.
- **Maladaptive narcissism** becomes exploitative, entitled, or unable to tolerate imperfection.
- At the far extreme lies **Narcissistic Personality Disorder (NPD)**, marked by pervasive grandiosity, need for admiration, and lack of empathy across all areas of life.

What Narcissism Is Not

- It is **not** ordinary confidence, ambition, or assertiveness.
- It is **not** setting boundaries or declining to please others.
- It is **not** a single selfish act.

Calling every unpleasant or arrogant person a narcissist cheapens the word and blinds us to the real condition, which is painful for the person who has it and difficult for those around them.

Recognizing the Pattern

True narcissistic behavior shows recurring themes:

- **Fragile self-image.** Small criticism feels like humiliation.
- **Manipulative validation-seeking.** Flattery and control used to sustain worth.
- **Empathy gaps.** Others are valued for utility, not individuality.
- **Idealize/devalue cycles.** Admiration turns to contempt when others fail to mirror perfection.

The pattern persists over years, not hours. A single argument or boast does not make someone narcissistic.

Healthy Self-Esteem vs. Narcissistic Defense

Healthy Self-Esteem	Narcissistic Pattern
"I'm worthy even when I fail."	"I'm worthless unless I succeed."
Flexible and reality-based.	Inflated but fragile.
Accepts feedback.	Interprets feedback as attack.
Values others as equals.	Sees others as mirrors or threats.

Living or Working with Narcissistic Patterns

Dealing with narcissism requires boundaries, not battles.

- **Stay factual.** Arguing emotion for emotion fuels defensiveness.
- **Set limits clearly and calmly.** Over-explaining invites manipulation.
- **Don't chase validation.** You won't out-convince insecurity.
- **Protect empathy.** See the fear beneath the arrogance, but don't excuse harm.

If you're in a close relationship with someone who meets the clinical pattern, professional counseling or support groups (for partners or families) can help you protect your own emotional stability.

Reflection Exercise

Think of a time when you labeled someone "narcissistic."

- What specific behavior triggered that label?
- Was it a pattern or a single incident?
- Could it have been insecurity, stress, or a different communication style?

This exercise helps separate perception from pathology.

Summary

Narcissism is not confidence out of control; it is insecurity on display.

Understanding it as a spectrum restores precision to the term and empathy to our judgments. Some people simply need reassurance; a few need treatment; all deserve clarity rather than caricature.

Chapter 3: Psychopathy and Sociopathy: Coldness vs. Chaos

Introduction

Psychopath and *sociopath* are usually misused words in the English language. They're tossed around in everyday speech to describe cruelty, manipulation, or indifference. In clinical and forensic psychology, however, these terms have precise meanings. They describe individuals who chronically violate social norms and the rights of others, not because they are angry or traumatized, but because their emotional wiring functions differently.

Both fall under the umbrella of **Antisocial Personality Disorder (ASPD)** in the *Diagnostic and Statistical Manual of Mental Disorders (DSM-5)*, but they represent different flavors of the same underlying condition: a lack of empathy paired with disregard for rules or consequences.

What Psychopathy Is

Psychopathy is defined by **emotional coldness** and **calculated manipulation**. Psychopaths tend to be calm, charming, and rational even while exploiting others. They rarely feel guilt or fear, and their emotional responses are shallow but well-performed. Their danger lies in their composure: they can read emotions without sharing them. Many are articulate and intelligent, excelling in environments that reward strategy and detachment.

Researchers often describe psychopaths as having a "low startle response" and diminished capacity for empathy; biological traits measurable in brain imaging and physiological studies.

What Sociopathy Is

Sociopathy describes the **volatile counterpart**. The sociopath has the same empathy deficit but poor impulse control. Instead of calculated manipulation, they react impulsively, often lashing out or breaking rules in the heat of emotion. They are prone to anger, risk-taking, and erratic behavior. Where the psychopath plots, the sociopath erupts.

Sociopaths often come from unstable or abusive environments; their patterns may arise from trauma and inconsistent socialization rather than innate neurology.

Key Differences

Trait	Psychopath	Sociopath
Emotional control	Cold, calculated	Impulsive, reactive
Empathy	Absent	Shallow, inconsistent
Planning	Strategic	Disorganized
Social mask	Charming, persuasive	Poorly maintained
Likelihood of violence	Lower but more planned	Higher but more chaotic

Both share chronic deceitfulness, disregard for others, and failure to learn from punishment.

Myths and Realities

Not all psychopaths are criminals. Many operate within legal systems, in business, politics, or high-risk professions, where fearlessness and charm are rewarded.

Not all criminals are psychopaths. Most crime results from circumstance, not innate pathology.

Psychopathy is rare. Estimates suggest about 1% of the general population meet criteria for clinical psychopathy.

Psychopath ≠ "evil." These are psychological conditions, not moral verdicts.

Dealing with Antisocial Patterns

When interacting with someone who shows persistent deceit, exploitation, or lack of remorse:

- **Set clear, enforceable boundaries.** Manipulative individuals test limits constantly.
- **Avoid emotional reasoning.** Logic and consistency protect you better than appeals to empathy.
- **Document agreements.** Verbal promises are easily distorted later.
- **Limit access to your vulnerabilities.** Oversharing provides ammunition.

If you must maintain contact (e.g., family or professional contexts), structured mediation or legal oversight is often necessary. If you can disengage safely, do so.

Reflection Exercise

Think about someone who has caused repeated harm or chaos.

- Did their actions seem impulsive or calculated?
- Were they capable of genuine remorse or empathy afterward?
- Could boundaries have protected you, or were they impossible to enforce?

The goal is not to label, but to recognize behavioral patterns so you can respond with clarity instead of confusion.

Summary

Psychopathy and sociopathy describe two forms of emotional blindness: one cool and strategic, the other hot and chaotic. Understanding them removes the false comfort of caricature. Most people you meet will have *traits* of self-interest or impulsivity, not full disorders. Recognizing the difference helps you stay compassionate toward imperfection while realistic about danger. The healthiest response is neither demonization nor denial, but informed self-protection.

Chapter 4: Borderline Personality Patterns: Intensity, Not Evil

Introduction

Few conditions are as misunderstood (or as unfairly stigmatized) as **Borderline Personality Disorder (BPD)**. The word *borderline* itself is an artifact of early psychiatry, when doctors believed the disorder existed "on the border" between neurosis and psychosis. We now understand it as a pattern of intense emotional reactivity, unstable relationships, and a fragile sense of self.

People with borderline traits don't lack empathy or morality. They feel *too much*, too fast, and too deeply, then struggle to regulate those feelings. Their lives often oscillate between idealization and despair, not from manipulation, but from fear of abandonment.

What Borderline Personality Disorder Is

BPD is a condition defined by **emotional dysregulation** — the inability to manage intense mood swings, often triggered by perceived rejection or instability.

Common patterns include:

- Rapid shifts between admiration and resentment toward the same person.
- Impulsive actions in response to emotional pain (spending, substance use, or self-harm).
- Chronic feelings of emptiness or identity confusion.
- Extreme fear of abandonment, sometimes leading to frantic attempts to prevent it.
- Periods of anger, guilt, or dissociation (feeling detached from oneself).

These reactions are not deliberate. They reflect a nervous system that interprets emotional threat as physical danger.

What It Is Not

BPD is not manipulativeness, cruelty, or "drama." Those are surface interpretations from people who experience the outbursts without seeing the underlying terror of loss. It is not a lack of empathy; in fact, many people with BPD are extraordinarily empathic but overwhelmed by their own feelings.

The disorder arises from a mix of **biological vulnerability** and **environmental trauma,** often early neglect, inconsistent care, or emotional invalidation. It is a condition of *injury*, not of intent.

The Emotional Landscape

Imagine feeling your emotions with the volume turned up to ten: joy becomes euphoria, sadness becomes despair, criticism becomes betrayal. That's the lived experience of BPD. Emotional intensity makes relationships both intoxicating and perilous. The individual craves closeness but fears engulfment, pushing others away to test loyalty, then pulling them back to avoid abandonment.

To outsiders, this looks like manipulation; to the person living it, it feels like survival.

Myths and Realities

Myth: "People with BPD can't be helped."
Reality: With structured therapy, especially Dialectical Behavior Therapy (DBT), outcomes are among the most promising in psychiatry.
Myth: "They're abusive or dangerous."
Reality: Most harm themselves emotionally or physically far more often than they harm others.
Myth: "They crave drama."
Reality: They crave connection and stability but don't yet know how to achieve it safely.

Living or Working with Borderline Patterns

If someone in your life shows these traits:

- **Maintain calm consistency.** Predictable reactions help regulate theirs.
- **Don't reward extremes.** Compassion works better than indulgence.
- **Set gentle but firm boundaries.** They may test them, but consistency builds trust.
- **Avoid labeling or moralizing.** Treat outbursts as distress, not defiance.
- **Encourage professional help.** Therapy (especially DBT, CBT, and schema therapy) can teach emotion-regulation skills that transform outcomes.

Supporting someone with BPD requires patience, but recovery and long-term stability are absolutely possible.

Reflection Exercise

Think of someone whose emotional reactions have felt overwhelming or unpredictable.

- What fears might lie beneath those reactions?
- How could consistency, rather than criticism, change the dynamic?
- Have you ever reacted from fear in ways that confused others?

This exercise helps transform judgment into empathy while preserving personal boundaries.

Summary

Borderline Personality Disorder is not "evil"; it's emotional vulnerability turned inward and outward simultaneously. The person who loves too hard and lashes out too fast is not scheming, they're hurting. Understanding this distinction allows compassion without enabling, distance without cruelty, and recognition that healing comes through structure, therapy, and time.

When you stop seeing "drama" and start seeing *pain*, you can respond with both firmness and kindness. The combination that makes recovery possible.

Chapter 5: The Culture of Labels

Introduction

Psychological language has escaped the clinic and entered everyday speech. Words like *toxic*, *narcissist*, *bipolar*, and *sociopath* are used as insults, diagnoses, and shorthand for "someone who frustrates me." This democratization of psychology has benefits (more awareness, more openness to mental-health discussion) but it also breeds confusion: when complex clinical concepts are reduced to social media catchphrases, empathy erodes and understanding collapses into caricature.

The purpose of this workbook is not to give you ammunition for judging others. It's to give you language precise enough to describe human behavior without turning observation into accusation.

How Label Culture Took Hold

The internet rewards simplicity and outrage. Psychological terms offer both: they sound authoritative and provide moral certainty. Calling someone a narcissist ends a conversation; it spares us the discomfort of ambiguity. But psychology, when practiced responsibly, is the study of *ambiguity*. It recognizes that motive, history, and biology interact in ways no meme can summarize.

Over time, mass culture has traded **diagnosis for dismissal**. Instead of "I'm hurt by this behavior," we say "You're a narcissist." Instead of "I'm anxious," we say "I have OCD." The result is a society fluent in labels but illiterate in nuance.

The Real Cost of Mislabeling

Misusing psychological terms damages everyone involved.

- It **invalidates** those who truly live with these conditions, making their experiences seem exaggerated.
- It **blocks communication**, replacing curiosity with certainty.
- It **distorts accountability**: people excuse cruelty as "just my trauma" or condemn assertiveness as "abuse."

Once a label is applied, discussion stops. The person becomes the diagnosis.

True psychological literacy begins with restraint: knowing when *not* to use a label.

Why We Reach for Labels

Humans name things to feel safe. Labels give the illusion of control: if we can define it, we can defend against it. But people are not fixed entities. Personality and pathology both exist on spectrums that shift with context and time. Labeling freezes motion; understanding restores it.

A healthy approach asks, *What pattern am I observing? What might it mean?* not *What category does this person belong to?*

How to Talk About Behavior Responsibly

Describe actions, not identities. Say "He often ignores others' input," not "He's a narcissist."

Use clinical terms only when clinically relevant. Outside diagnosis or education, they're usually unnecessary.

Distinguish harm from difference. A person can frustrate you without being disordered.

Be curious before being certain. Ask what function the behavior serves — protection, fear, habit, or belief.

Precision in language creates precision in empathy.

A Better Vocabulary for Everyday Life

Instead of pathologizing, use neutral behavioral descriptors:

- controlling → *prefers structure*
- avoidant → *withdraws when stressed*
- manipulative → *uses persuasion to meet needs*
- narcissistic → *seeks validation to feel secure*

This vocabulary invites conversation rather than condemnation.

Reflection Exercise

Recall a time you used or heard a psychological label in casual conversation.

- What behavior was the label trying to explain?
- Could a more neutral description have worked better?
- How might your view of the person change if you replaced the label with context?

Write a few sentences reframing that situation in plain, non-clinical language. The goal is not political correctness — it's accuracy.

Summary

Psychological language should illuminate, not weaponize. Labels are tools, not truths. Use them to understand patterns, not to freeze people inside them. The more precisely you speak, the more compassion you can afford.

In the end, the measure of psychological literacy is simple: it's not how many terms you know, but how gently you use them.

Part III: Personality and Mental Health

Chapter 1: Healthy Personality vs. Mental Disorder

Introduction

Personality describes the *enduring pattern* of thoughts, feelings, and behaviors that make you recognizable across time. A mental disorder describes when those patterns (or any part of your emotional or cognitive life) cause significant distress or impairment. The difference lies not in the *kind* of feeling or trait, but in its **intensity, persistence, and impact**.

Everyone experiences anxiety, sadness, impulsivity, or self-doubt. In healthy personality, these come and go; they adapt to circumstance. In mental disorder, they persist regardless of circumstance and begin to narrow life rather than enrich it.

Flexibility vs. Rigidity

The surest sign of psychological health is **flexibility,** the ability to adjust behavior to fit reality.

A healthy introvert can still socialize when necessary. A healthy perfectionist can still accept "good enough." A healthy empath can still say no.

Mental disorder reduces flexibility. Thoughts become repetitive, emotions disproportionate, and actions compulsive. The person no longer *has* moods and fears—they are *had by* them.

Think of personality as a riverbed and mental illness as a flood that escapes it. The river's shape remains, but control is lost.

Function, Not Fault

Clinical psychology avoids moral language. A disorder is not "bad behavior" but a **functional impairment**—something that limits a person's ability to live, love, and work effectively. It's diagnosed only when symptoms:

Cause significant distress to the individual or others, **and**

Interfere with major areas of life such as relationships, employment, or self-care.

Feeling sad is human; being unable to get out of bed for weeks is depression. Being meticulous is preference; being unable to leave home until every object is aligned is compulsion.

How Personality and Mental Health Interact

Your personality influences *how* you experience illness, but not necessarily *whether* you develop one.

- An anxious personality might catastrophize physical sensations, leading to panic attacks.
- A perfectionistic thinker might mask depression until exhaustion breaks through.
- A spontaneous, novelty-seeking type might struggle with ADHD symptoms more visibly.

Healthy self-awareness lets you recognize these vulnerabilities early and adapt your coping strategies to fit your style.

The Gray Zone: Traits vs. Disorders

Most people live in the gray zone between "fine" and "diagnosable." A few examples illustrate the difference:

Everyday Trait	Clinical Disorder
Preference for order	Obsessive-Compulsive Disorder (repetitive rituals and intrusive thoughts)
Shyness	Social Anxiety Disorder (avoidance causing isolation)
Moodiness	Bipolar Disorder (distinct manic and depressive episodes)
Distractibility	ADHD (neurological impairment of attention and impulse control)

Traits are descriptive; disorders are disabling. The line is drawn where function erodes.

When to Seek Professional Help

It's time to consult a mental-health professional when:

- Emotional states dominate most days and seem impossible to change alone.
- Behavior repeatedly damages work, health, or relationships despite effort.
- Coping methods revolve around numbing (alcohol, overeating, compulsive scrolling).
- Friends or family express concern that you no longer seem like yourself.

Early intervention is not a sign of weakness; it's maintenance, like seeing a doctor for high blood pressure before a heart attack.

Reflection Exercise

Identify one recurring pattern in yourself that sometimes helps and sometimes hurts.

- When does it serve you?

- When does it start running you?
- What small adjustment might restore flexibility?

This self-check distinguishes *personality expression* from *symptom intrusion*.

Summary

Healthy personality adapts; disordered functioning persists. The line between them isn't moral but practical: does this pattern make life larger or smaller? Understanding that difference prepares you to explore the specific conditions in the chapters that follow—depression, anxiety, bipolar disorder, ADHD, OCD, autism, and others—with accuracy and empathy.

Chapter 2: Mood and Emotional Disorders

Introduction

Mood disorders are among the most common and most misunderstood mental-health conditions. Nearly everyone experiences sadness, stress, or mood swings — but disorders like **Depression**, **Bipolar Disorder**, and **Anxiety Disorders** go beyond ordinary emotion. They persist, distort perception, and interfere with daily life.

A mood disorder doesn't mean someone is weak or undisciplined; it means their brain's regulation of mood and energy has gone off-balance. With treatment and awareness, recovery is not only possible — it's common.

Depression: More Than Sadness

What It Is

Depression (Major Depressive Disorder) is a medical condition that alters how a person feels, thinks, and functions. It lasts weeks or months, not days, and doesn't always follow a life event. It often appears quietly — a slow withdrawal from pleasure, motivation, or hope.

Common symptoms include:

Persistent sadness or emptiness

Loss of interest in activities once enjoyed

Fatigue or lack of concentration

Sleep or appetite changes

Feelings of guilt, worthlessness, or hopelessness

Thoughts of death or suicide

Depression can mimic personality traits. A normally cheerful person may seem "lazy" or "disengaged." A perfectionist may become hypercritical of themselves. The key is *duration and dysfunction* — when the fog doesn't lift despite effort.

What It Is Not

It's not simply grief, bad days, or pessimism. Everyone feels low at times, but depression is a shutdown of the emotional system, not a temporary dip. No amount of "cheering up" or "thinking positive" fixes a brain that has lost its chemical equilibrium.

What Helps

Therapy (especially cognitive-behavioral or interpersonal therapy), antidepressant medication, consistent sleep, physical activity, and social connection all help restore stability. The combination varies by person, but treatment works — and seeking it is a sign of self-respect, not failure.

Bipolar Disorder: The Cycle of Highs and Lows

What It Is

Bipolar Disorder is characterized by alternating periods of **depression** and **mania** (or its milder form, **hypomania**). The shifts are not ordinary mood swings; they involve dramatic changes in energy, sleep, judgment, and confidence.

During **mania**, a person may feel euphoric, need little sleep, talk rapidly, or make reckless choices (spending sprees, impulsive travel, grandiose plans). In **depression**, energy and hope crash, sometimes leading to despair.

There are two main types:

- **Bipolar I** – at least one full manic episode, often alternating with depression.
- **Bipolar II** – hypomanic episodes alternating with major depression (the highs are milder, the lows often deeper).

What It Is Not

It's not moodiness, volatility, or emotional "drama." True mania is physiological: the brain shifts into overdrive. People often feel unstoppable — until exhaustion or consequences follow.

What Helps

Mood stabilizers (such as lithium or lamotrigine), therapy, and lifestyle consistency (sleep, diet, structure) are key. Unmanaged bipolar disorder can mimic success temporarily — creativity surges, productivity spikes — but stability, not intensity, sustains health.

The Creative Connection

Some of history's most brilliant artists, scientists, and writers are believed to have had bipolar disorder. But romanticizing it is dangerous. Creativity flourishes best when the mind is stable enough to finish what inspiration begins.

Anxiety Disorders: The Mind's False Alarms

What It Is

Anxiety is a natural alarm system, keeping us alert to danger. In an anxiety disorder, that system misfires, sending constant or disproportionate signals of threat. The body reacts as if under attack — even during ordinary events like answering a phone call or entering a store.

Common anxiety disorders include:

- **Generalized Anxiety Disorder (GAD):** chronic worry, muscle tension, insomnia, restlessness.
- **Panic Disorder:** sudden waves of intense fear, often mistaken for heart attacks.
- **Social Anxiety Disorder:** fear of embarrassment or judgment in social settings.

- **Phobias:** intense fear of specific situations or objects.
- **Physical Symptoms:** racing heart, sweating, dizziness, stomach pain, shortness of breath — all real, even when no external danger exists.

What It Is Not

Anxiety is not "being nervous" or "overthinking." It's not a lack of willpower. The brain's threat-detection network (amygdala and prefrontal cortex) has become hyper-reactive. Logical reassurance alone can't override the body's physiological alarm once it's triggered.

What Helps

Treatment often combines therapy (especially cognitive-behavioral therapy, mindfulness, or exposure therapy), medication (SSRIs, beta-blockers), and grounding techniques (slow breathing, progressive relaxation). Avoidance temporarily eases anxiety but strengthens it long-term; facing fears safely, under guidance, reduces it.

When Emotions Become Disorders

Everyone experiences sadness, excitement, and worry — these are normal emotional weather patterns. Mood disorders are *climate*, not weather. They linger and reshape the landscape of thought.

A key test:

Does the feeling match the situation, or has it outlasted it?

If emotions persist when life has changed, or if they feel uncontrollable and constant, professional evaluation can help determine whether a mood disorder is present.

Reflection Exercise

Think of an emotional state that recurs for you — sadness, anger, anxiety, or restlessness.
How long does it usually last?
What restores balance?
Has it ever limited your ability to function or connect with others?
Write down what helps most when you recover. That list becomes your personalized "early warning system" for emotional imbalance.

Summary

Mood disorders are not personality flaws; they are disruptions in the brain's ability to regulate emotion. Recognizing them removes shame and opens doors to effective care. The goal isn't perpetual happiness — it's **emotional resilience**, the ability to feel fully without being ruled by feeling.

Chapter 3: Neurodevelopmental Conditions

Introduction

Some differences in behavior and cognition don't arise from mood or personality, but from the way the brain itself develops and processes information. These are called **neurodevelopmental conditions** — variations in brain structure and function that appear early in life and persist into adulthood.

Two of the most widely discussed are **Autism Spectrum Disorder (ASD)** and **Attention-Deficit/Hyperactivity Disorder (ADHD)**. Both affect attention, communication, and sensory processing, but in distinct ways. They are not diseases to be "cured," nor character flaws to be "corrected." They are alternative wiring patterns that shape how a person perceives and engages with the world.

Autism Spectrum Disorder (ASD)

What It Is

Autism is a **neurological difference** affecting how individuals interpret social cues, language, and sensory information. It's called a *spectrum* because expression ranges widely — from people who need substantial daily support to those who live independently and succeed in complex professions.

Common characteristics include:

- Differences in eye contact, tone, or social reciprocity
- Focused or intense interests
- Preference for routine and predictability
- Heightened or reduced sensory sensitivity (to sound, light, touch, taste)
- Literal or precise communication style
- Exceptional memory or pattern-recognition skills

Autism is fundamentally about **processing**, not emotion. Many autistic individuals experience deep empathy but express it differently — often through problem-solving, advocacy, or action rather than overt emotional display.

What It Is Not

Autism is not intellectual disability, lack of empathy, or "coldness." It does not mean someone is trapped in their own world; it means they experience the shared world through a different set of filters.

It is not caused by parenting style, vaccines, or social media — all disproven myths. It's a neurobiological variation influenced by genetics and early brain development.

What Helps

Support focuses on adaptation, not normalization:

Clear communication and predictable structure reduce sensory and social overload.

Occupational or speech therapy can build practical skills.

Acceptance and inclusion foster mental health far better than attempts to "mask" difference.

The guiding principle is **neurodiversity** — recognizing that varied cognitive styles enrich, rather than diminish, humanity.

Attention-Deficit/Hyperactivity Disorder (ADHD)

What It Is

ADHD is a **neurobiological regulation disorder** involving differences in dopamine and norepinephrine pathways that affect attention, impulse control, and working memory. It's not a failure to pay attention — it's difficulty directing attention on demand.

Key symptoms appear in childhood and may persist into adulthood:

- Inattention (easily distracted, forgetful, difficulty finishing tasks)
- Hyperactivity (restlessness, constant movement or fidgeting)
- Impulsivity (blurting out, interrupting, acting before thinking)

Adults with ADHD often describe it as having too many browser tabs open — all playing sound at once.

What It Is Not

It's not laziness, immaturity, or a discipline problem. People with ADHD can focus intensely on tasks that interest them (*hyperfocus*), but struggle with tasks lacking stimulation. It's a mismatch between brain chemistry and environment, not motivation.

What Helps

Evidence-based treatment combines:

- **Medication** (stimulant or non-stimulant) to regulate neurotransmitters
- **Behavioral strategies** to structure time and minimize distractions
- **Coaching or therapy** to build organization and emotional regulation
- **Sleep, exercise, and consistent routines** to stabilize attention

Untreated ADHD can cause chronic frustration, underachievement, and low self-esteem. Managed ADHD often becomes a strength — fostering creativity, spontaneity, and resilience.

Neurodiversity and Society

Historically, neurodevelopmental differences were pathologized. Today, the **neurodiversity movement** reframes them as natural variations within the human population. The goal is not to romanticize disability but to recognize that support, not shame, determines outcome.

A world designed only for neurotypical minds excludes valuable perspectives. When workplaces, schools, and communities allow flexible communication, sensory accommodations, and task variety, neurodivergent people often excel.

Reflection Exercise

Think of a person — perhaps yourself — who processes the world differently.

How might that difference be a strength in some settings but a challenge in others?

What could you change (in environment, communication, or expectation) to make collaboration easier?

How does reframing "deficit" as "difference" alter your empathy?

Summary

Neurodevelopmental conditions are not deviations from normality but expressions of human variety. Autism and ADHD show that brains can organize attention, perception, and emotion in multiple valid ways. The goal is understanding, not correction — to build systems flexible enough for every kind of mind.

Chapter 4: Obsessive-Compulsive Disorder and Related Patterns

Introduction

Few conditions are more misrepresented in popular speech than **Obsessive-Compulsive Disorder (OCD)**. People often say, "I'm so OCD," when they mean they like things tidy or dislike mistakes. True OCD is not about preference or neatness — it is about **intrusion and compulsion**: unwanted thoughts that provoke anxiety and rituals performed to relieve it.

It is a disorder of *control*, not cleanliness — the mind's attempt to manage fear through repetition.

What OCD Is

OCD consists of two linked elements:

- **Obsessions** – intrusive, unwanted thoughts, images, or urges that cause distress.
- **Compulsions** – repetitive behaviors or mental acts done to neutralize that distress.

Example: a person fears contamination (obsession), so they wash their hands repeatedly until the anxiety temporarily subsides (compulsion). The relief reinforces the ritual, locking the person into a cycle that consumes hours daily.

Common themes include:

- Fear of contamination or illness
- Fear of harming others by accident or negligence
- Religious or moral scrupulosity
- Symmetry, counting, or repeating rituals
- Intrusive violent or sexual images (rarely acted upon but deeply distressing)

The key feature is **recognition** — most people with OCD know their fears are irrational but feel powerless to stop.

What OCD Is Not

It is not a personality trait, nor a quirk of perfectionism. It is not an "attention to detail" habit, nor a form of anxiety that can be rationalized away. It's also distinct from **Obsessive-Compulsive Personality Disorder (OCPD)**, which describes a rigid need for order and control but without intrusive thoughts or ritualized relief.

OCD is driven by fear, not preference. The compulsions relieve anxiety briefly but make it worse over time.

What Helps

- **Evidence-based treatments** are highly effective:

- **Exposure and Response Prevention (ERP)** therapy gradually reduces anxiety by allowing exposure to feared thoughts while resisting rituals.
- **Cognitive-Behavioral Therapy (CBT)** helps reframe distorted beliefs about responsibility and risk.
- **Medication** (usually SSRIs) can reduce the intensity of obsessions, giving therapy more traction.

Avoiding triggers feels safe in the short term but feeds the disorder. Successful treatment teaches that thoughts are not threats — they are mental noise, not moral verdicts.

The Spectrum of Control

Everyone has routines or habits that create comfort. The difference between orderliness and OCD lies in *flexibility*:

Healthy Routine	OCD Pattern
Optional and helpful	Compulsive and exhausting
Can skip without panic	Skipping causes intense anxiety
Serves function	Serves fear

When control stops serving you and starts owning you, it's time to seek help.

Related Conditions

OCD shares features with several other disorders that revolve around repetitive thoughts or behaviors:

- **Body Dysmorphic Disorder (BDD):** obsession with perceived physical flaws.
- **Hoarding Disorder:** difficulty discarding items, leading to unsafe clutter.
- **Trichotillomania (Hair-Pulling) and Skin-Picking Disorder:** repetitive grooming behaviors used to relieve tension.

These are sometimes called *Obsessive-Compulsive and Related Disorders* because they share similar brain circuits and treatment strategies.

Reflection Exercise

Think about an area of life where you value control — your home, appearance, work, or schedule.

Does that control reduce anxiety or increase it?

Could flexibility, even in small ways, bring relief rather than fear?

How do you react when control is disrupted?

Recognizing the difference between comfort and compulsion is the first step toward freedom.

Summary

Obsessive-Compulsive Disorder is not a personality quirk; it's an anxiety loop disguised as control. People with OCD aren't perfectionists — they're often terrified of imperfection. Understanding this distinction transforms judgment into empathy and replaces shame with strategy. OCD is treatable, and recovery doesn't mean abandoning order — it means reclaiming peace from fear.

Chapter 5: Related Disorders: Body Image, Hoarding, and Repetitive Behaviors

Introduction

The mind can become trapped in repetitive loops that look voluntary but aren't. These disorders—**Body Dysmorphic Disorder (BDD)**, **Eating Disorders (Anorexia and Bulimia)**, **Hoarding Disorder**, and **Body-Focused Repetitive Behaviors**—share features with Obsessive-Compulsive Disorder (OCD). They involve intrusive thoughts, rituals, and intense anxiety when those rituals are broken. Though their themes differ—appearance, food, possessions, or bodily tension—the underlying mechanism is the same: control becomes compulsion.

Body Dysmorphic Disorder (BDD)

What It Is

BDD centers on obsessive preoccupation with perceived physical flaws, often minor or invisible to others. The person believes they look deformed, asymmetrical, or unattractive and spends hours checking mirrors, grooming, or comparing themselves to others.

Common patterns include mirror-checking, reassurance-seeking, and repeated cosmetic procedures that never bring relief.

The distress arises not from the body itself but from the **belief** that something is wrong with it.

What It Is Not

BDD is not vanity or insecurity. Everyone worries about appearance occasionally; in BDD the worry dominates life.

What Helps

Cognitive-Behavioral Therapy (especially Exposure and Response Prevention) and certain antidepressants (SSRIs) can significantly reduce obsessional thinking. Cosmetic surgery almost never helps; psychological treatment addresses the real distortion — perception, not flesh.

Eating Disorders: Anorexia and Bulimia

What They Are

Eating disorders occupy the same body-image continuum as BDD but add life-threatening physiological risk. They are illnesses of **control, identity, and self-worth** expressed through food and weight.

Anorexia Nervosa

Marked by severe food restriction, intense fear of gaining weight, and distorted body image, anorexia leads to dangerous malnutrition and often denial of illness. The individual may see themselves as overweight despite visible emaciation. Perfectionism and a need for certainty frequently underlie the disorder; hunger becomes proof of discipline, control, and purity.

Bulimia Nervosa

Bulimia involves cycles of binge eating followed by compensatory behaviors such as vomiting, fasting, or excessive exercise. The binge provides brief relief from emotional pain; the purge restores a sense of control. The physical consequences can be severe—electrolyte imbalance, dental erosion, gastrointestinal damage—but the emotional suffering is equally intense.

What They Are Not

They are not diets gone too far, vanity projects, or choices. They are psychiatric and medical conditions with the highest mortality rate among mental illnesses.

What Helps

Recovery requires multidisciplinary care:

- **Medical monitoring** to restore physical stability.
- **Nutritional therapy** to rebuild balanced eating.
- **Psychotherapy**—especially Cognitive-Behavioral Therapy (CBT-E) or Family-Based Treatment (FBT).
- **Medication** may support co-occurring anxiety or depression.

Full recovery is possible, but secrecy sustains illness; openness and early intervention save lives.

Hoarding Disorder

What It Is

Hoarding involves persistent difficulty discarding possessions—regardless of value—because doing so causes intense anxiety or guilt. Over time, living spaces become cluttered to the point of dysfunction: unusable kitchens, blocked doors, unsafe conditions.

The behavior often stems from fear of waste, emotional attachment to objects, or the belief that each item might someday be needed. To the hoarder, each possession carries meaning, history, or identity.

What It Is Not

It's not simple messiness, collecting, or laziness. Collectors organize and display; hoarders accumulate and conceal. The difference is control—collecting adds pleasure, hoarding adds paralysis.

What Helps

Effective treatment includes Cognitive-Behavioral Therapy tailored for hoarding, sometimes combined with medication to reduce anxiety and indecision. Support from family or community services can help restore safety, but forced cleanup without therapy often triggers relapse.

Compassionate patience matters: every object represents more than material; it represents memory and fear.

Body-Focused Repetitive Behaviors (BFRBs)

These include:
Trichotillomania – recurrent hair-pulling from scalp, eyebrows, or other areas.
Excoriation (Skin-Picking) Disorder – compulsive picking of skin leading to sores or scarring.

What They Are

BFRBs are tension-relief behaviors. The act temporarily soothes anxiety or boredom but quickly leads to shame and concealment. Many people describe entering a "trance" or "automatic" state before realizing they've pulled or picked.

What They Are Not

They are not attention-seeking or self-harm in the traditional sense. Most individuals with BFRBs wish desperately to stop. Stress, fatigue, and sensory sensitivity often trigger episodes.

What Helps

Habit Reversal Training (HRT): teaches awareness of triggers and substitutes new responses (e.g., squeezing a stress ball).
Cognitive-Behavioral Therapy (CBT): addresses perfectionism, shame, and avoidance.
Medication: sometimes used to reduce impulse severity.
Gentle self-compassion is crucial—shame fuels the cycle; acceptance weakens it.

Common Threads

All these disorders share: intrusive preoccupation, temporary relief through ritual, and growing impairment over time. They are not moral failings but maladaptive attempts to soothe distress through control.

Reflection Exercise

Think about an area where control provides comfort—appearance, order, or possessions. When does it feel empowering, and when oppressive?

What emotion hides underneath: fear, shame, or helplessness?

Understanding motive begins the process of recovery.

Summary

Body-image and control-related disorders—BDD, anorexia, bulimia, hoarding, and BFRBs—show how the mind can turn ordinary self-care into compulsion. The answer is not discipline but compassion guided by evidence-based treatment. Control is regained not by tightening the grip, but by learning to loosen it safely.

Chapter 6: Psychotic and Thought Disorders

Introduction

Few mental-health conditions carry as much misunderstanding as the **psychotic disorders**. Popular culture often portrays "psychosis" as violence or madness. In reality, these disorders are primarily about **perception and interpretation** — the way the mind constructs reality.

Psychosis occurs when that construction becomes unstable. People may see, hear, or believe things that others do not. These experiences are not moral failings or signs of weak will. They are symptoms of a brain that has temporarily lost the ability to distinguish between inner thought and outer reality.

Understanding psychotic disorders requires curiosity instead of fear, because treatment and recovery are both possible.

What Psychosis Is

Psychosis is a **symptom**, not a diagnosis. It refers to a state in which perception, thought, or emotion become detached from reality. Common features include:

- **Hallucinations:** sensory experiences without external stimuli (hearing voices, seeing visions, feeling sensations that aren't there).
- **Delusions:** firmly held false beliefs resistant to contrary evidence (believing one is being watched, poisoned, or specially chosen for a mission).
- **Disorganized thinking or speech:** words or ideas that lose logical order.
- **Flattened or inappropriate emotion:** expressions don't match context or vanish altogether.

Psychosis can appear in several disorders, including **Schizophrenia**, **Schizoaffective Disorder**, **Bipolar Disorder**, **Severe Depression**, or even temporary conditions caused by **substance use**, **sleep deprivation**, or **medical illness**.

Schizophrenia: The Prototype Disorder

What It Is

Schizophrenia is a chronic disorder marked by persistent psychosis and cognitive changes. It typically begins in late adolescence or early adulthood and affects about 1% of the population worldwide.

Core symptoms fall into three categories:

- **Positive symptoms** (added experiences): hallucinations, delusions, disorganized speech or behavior.
- **Negative symptoms** (loss of normal function): reduced motivation, flat affect, social withdrawal.

- **Cognitive symptoms:** difficulty concentrating, remembering, or planning.

What It Is Not

Schizophrenia is not "split personality." That's a separate condition (Dissociative Identity Disorder). Nor does schizophrenia automatically imply danger. With modern treatment, most individuals can live stable, productive lives.

What Helps

- **Antipsychotic medication** (newer "atypical" drugs) reduces hallucinations and delusions.
- **Psychosocial therapy** improves communication and daily functioning.
- **Supportive housing and vocational programs** reduce relapse.

Early, continuous treatment is the strongest predictor of good outcomes.

Schizoaffective Disorder

This condition bridges schizophrenia and mood disorders. People experience both psychotic symptoms (hallucinations or delusions) and major mood episodes (depression or mania). It's diagnosed when psychotic symptoms persist beyond the mood episodes themselves.

Treatment combines **antipsychotic** and **mood-stabilizing** medication along with therapy, addressing both dimensions of the illness. When properly managed, individuals often maintain work, relationships, and independence.

Delusional Disorder

Delusional Disorder involves one or more non-bizarre delusions — beliefs that could be possible in real life but aren't (e.g., being secretly loved by a public figure, or being followed). Unlike schizophrenia, functioning outside the delusional theme may remain intact.

It's rare but challenging because those affected rarely see their beliefs as irrational. Treatment focuses on trust-building, gentle reality testing, and long-term therapy.

Causes and Risk Factors

Psychotic disorders arise from a combination of:

- **Genetics:** family history increases vulnerability but is not destiny.
- **Neurobiology:** dopamine dysregulation and structural brain differences contribute.
- **Stress and trauma:** can trigger or exacerbate symptoms in predisposed individuals.
- **Substance use:** particularly cannabis and stimulants, can induce or worsen psychosis.

The "stress–vulnerability model" explains it best: biology provides the match; stress provides the spark.

Recovery and Management

Contrary to popular myth, many people with psychotic disorders recover or manage their symptoms effectively. Stability depends on early diagnosis, adherence to treatment, and strong social support. Stigma remains the greatest barrier — preventing individuals from seeking help until symptoms worsen.

The right combination of **medication, therapy, structure, and purpose** can restore not just functioning, but dignity and meaning.

Reflection Exercise

Think about a film or story that portrayed psychosis.
What emotions did it evoke — fear, pity, curiosity?
How accurate was the portrayal compared to what you've learned here?
How might greater understanding replace fear with compassion in real life?

Summary

Psychotic and thought disorders remind us how fragile and wondrous the mind's reality-building machinery can be. These are not moral or character defects; they are medical conditions affecting perception. When society replaces stigma with understanding, those who experience psychosis gain not only treatment but acceptance — and the chance to live full, meaningful lives within their communities.

Chapter 7: Trauma and Stressor-Related Disorders

Introduction

Trauma reshapes the way the mind and body perceive safety. After overwhelming events, the nervous system can remain locked in survival mode — hyperalert, anxious, easily startled, or emotionally numb. This state isn't weakness or dramatization; it's physiology.

Disorders related to trauma arise when that survival response fails to quiet after danger has passed. They include **Post-Traumatic Stress Disorder (PTSD)**, **Complex PTSD (C-PTSD)**, and **Adjustment Disorders**. Each describes the mind's effort to live with what was once unbearable.

Post-Traumatic Stress Disorder (PTSD)

What It Is

PTSD develops after direct or vicarious exposure to life-threatening or deeply distressing events — combat, assault, disasters, severe accidents, or abuse. The hallmark is re-experiencing the trauma as though it is still happening.

Core symptom clusters:

- **Intrusion:** flashbacks, nightmares, intrusive memories.
- **Avoidance:** steering clear of reminders (people, places, sounds).
- **Hyperarousal:** exaggerated startle, irritability, insomnia, vigilance.
- **Negative changes in mood and cognition:** guilt, emotional numbing, detachment.

The brain's fear circuitry (amygdala, hippocampus) remains overactive, flooding the body with stress hormones at harmless cues — a slammed door, a certain smell, a phrase.

What It Is Not

PTSD is not an overreaction or failure to "move on." It is the body's learned alarm system refusing to stand down.

What Helps

Evidence-based treatments include:

- **Trauma-Focused Cognitive-Behavioral Therapy (TF-CBT)**
- **Eye-Movement Desensitization and Reprocessing (EMDR)**
- **Prolonged Exposure Therapy (PE)**
- **Medication** for sleep and anxiety regulation (SSRIs, prazosin)

Healing depends on restoring a sense of safety in the body as well as in the mind — grounding, breath work, and supportive relationships are central.

Complex PTSD (C-PTSD)

What It Is

C-PTSD arises from **chronic or repeated trauma** — prolonged abuse, captivity, neglect, or domination. Unlike PTSD, which centers on a single event, C-PTSD involves years of conditioning in fear and helplessness.

Symptoms overlap with PTSD but add:

- Persistent shame or guilt
- Emotional flashbacks without clear memories
- Difficulty trusting or sustaining relationships
- Identity disturbances ("I don't know who I am without the trauma")
- Self-destructive coping behaviors

C-PTSD blurs the line between trauma and personality, because it alters development itself. Survivors may see themselves not as people who *had* trauma, but as people *made* by it.

What Helps

Treatment focuses on **stabilization before processing**.

- Establishing safety and routine
- Learning emotional regulation (through Dialectical Behavior Therapy or somatic techniques)
- Gradual trauma processing once resilience builds

Recovery is slower but profoundly possible. The aim is integration, not erasure — transforming survival strategies into strengths.

Adjustment Disorders

What They Are

Adjustment Disorders describe excessive emotional or behavioral reactions to identifiable stressors — divorce, job loss, relocation, illness — that exceed normal adaptation but fall short of PTSD.

Symptoms may include anxiety, sadness, or behavioral change beginning within three months of the stressor and resolving within six.

These disorders highlight an important truth: **you don't need a catastrophe to struggle**. Even normal life changes can temporarily overwhelm coping capacity.

What Helps

Short-term psychotherapy emphasizing problem-solving, coping skills, and social support is typically effective. Most people recover fully once stability returns.

The Physiology of Trauma

Trauma resides in the nervous system, not just in memory. The "fight-flight-freeze" mechanism stays engaged, keeping muscles tense, heart rate elevated, and digestion impaired. The goal of treatment is to teach the body that the danger has passed — to *complete* the defensive response that was interrupted.

Reflection Exercise

Recall a time when a stressful event lingered longer than expected.
How did your body signal stress (sleep, appetite, tension)?
What eventually told your mind, "I'm safe again"?
Which coping methods calmed rather than numbed you?
Recognizing the body's language of safety is the cornerstone of trauma recovery.

Summary

Trauma is not what happens to us but what remains inside us afterward. PTSD, C-PTSD, and Adjustment Disorders are not marks of fragility but signs of survival systems working overtime. Healing comes from restoring safety, connection, and agency — the very things trauma once stole.

When we understand trauma as physiology, not character, compassion replaces stigma, and recovery becomes a process of teaching the body to live in peace with the mind again.

Chapter 8: Personality and the Brain: Biological and Cognitive Foundations

Introduction

Every thought, mood, and personality trait has a biological foundation. This doesn't mean personality is fixed by our genes, but that the *raw materials* of temperament—energy, reactivity, focus, sociability—emerge from the chemistry and architecture of the brain. Experience shapes those circuits over time, blending nature and nurture into what we call the self.

Understanding the brain's role in personality helps us see behavior not as moral success or failure, but as biology interacting with circumstance.

The Brain's Architecture of Personality

Different brain regions and networks cooperate to create what we experience as "personality." None work in isolation:

- **The Limbic System** — the emotional core, including the **amygdala** (fear and threat detection) and **hippocampus** (memory).
- **The Prefrontal Cortex** — the executive center; regulates planning, impulse control, and empathy.
- **The Anterior Cingulate Cortex** — monitors conflict and helps balance emotion and logic.
- **The Insula** — senses the internal state of the body, influencing intuition and self-awareness.

A person whose limbic system reacts quickly may appear passionate or anxious. Someone with highly efficient prefrontal regulation may seem calm, focused, and disciplined. Neither is "better" — they represent different biological strategies for survival.

Neurochemistry and Temperament

Brain chemicals, or neurotransmitters, influence personality's tone and pace:

- **Dopamine** fuels motivation, curiosity, and reward-seeking. High dopamine activity is linked to novelty and creativity; low levels can accompany depression or apathy.
- **Serotonin** stabilizes mood and inhibits impulsivity. Balanced serotonin supports patience and social cooperation; imbalance can lead to anxiety or mood fluctuation.
- **Norepinephrine** drives alertness and energy. Too much creates agitation; too little causes sluggishness.
- **GABA** calms the nervous system; **glutamate** excites it. Personality reflects their balance — some people naturally idle high, others low.

In effect, our personalities are symphonies played by neurotransmitters. Therapy, medication, mindfulness, and lifestyle adjustments tune the instruments, not replace them.

Genetics vs. Environment: The Twin Equation

Twin and adoption studies reveal that **about 40–60%** of personality variance is heritable. The rest comes from environment — family dynamics, culture, trauma, education, and random experience.

Genes provide a range; environment decides where within that range we live.

Think of genetics as *ink color* and environment as *paper texture*: both shape what the writing looks like, but neither determines the story.

Cognition and Perception: The Brain as Interpreter

The brain doesn't record reality; it interprets it. Cognitive psychology shows that personality partly reflects *interpretive bias* — the habitual way we filter information:

- **Optimists** notice opportunity before threat.
- **Neurotics** notice risk before safety.
- **Introverts** process stimuli deeply, sometimes to overload.
- **Extroverts** seek stimulation to maintain engagement.

Each bias has adaptive value. Problems arise only when the filter becomes rigid — when anxiety, depression, or trauma narrow perception until flexibility is lost.

Plasticity: The Brain Can Change

Neuroscience once assumed the adult brain was static. We now know it's **plastic** — capable of rewiring through experience, therapy, learning, and even deliberate thought.

- **Mindfulness and meditation** thicken the prefrontal cortex, improving emotional regulation.
- **Cognitive-behavioral therapy (CBT)** literally reshapes neural pathways by replacing fear-based thought loops with realistic ones.
- **Exercise and sleep** enhance neurogenesis (new neuron growth).

This means personality, though rooted in biology, can evolve through effort and environment. You are not merely your wiring; you are your wiring plus what you do with it.

When Biology Becomes Vulnerability

Certain traits predispose people to mental health challenges:

- High emotional reactivity → anxiety or mood disorders.
- Low dopamine responsiveness → depression or apathy.
- Impulsivity → addiction or ADHD.

These are tendencies, not destinies. Awareness allows preemptive self-care—choosing environments and habits that match your wiring rather than punish it.

Reflection Exercise

List three aspects of yourself you once judged harshly — restlessness, sensitivity, stubbornness, perfectionism.

How might each reflect an underlying biological strength (energy, empathy, persistence, attention to detail)?

How could you manage them so they serve rather than sabotage you?

Understanding your biology reframes self-criticism as self-knowledge.

Summary

Personality is the conversation between the brain and the world. Genes start the sentence; experience finishes it. The brain's chemistry explains our tendencies, but consciousness allows choice. By knowing our neurological blueprint, we learn not to fight our wiring but to master it — turning predisposition into potential.

Chapter 9: Personality in Context: Culture, Upbringing, and Society

Introduction

Personality never develops in isolation. Every trait is shaped, amplified, or suppressed by context—family expectations, cultural norms, social hierarchies, and the lessons experience teaches about power and safety. You might be born with the wiring for optimism or assertiveness, but environment decides whether those qualities are encouraged or punished.

Culture writes the operating manual for temperament. Where the individual ends and the environment begins is never clear.

Upbringing: The First Laboratory of Personality

Early family life is the testing ground for emotional habits.

- **Authoritative households** (warm but structured) tend to produce secure, self-regulated personalities.
- **Authoritarian households** (strict, punitive) often yield either compliance or rebellion—two sides of learned fear.
- **Permissive environments** can foster creativity but may hinder impulse control.
- **Neglectful or chaotic homes** teach hypervigilance and mistrust, shaping later anxiety or avoidance.

In these formative years, a child learns two fundamental truths: *What happens when I act?* and *Am I safe when I do?* The answers to those questions echo throughout adulthood.

Culture: The Invisible Personality

Cultures differ dramatically in how they value individuality, emotion, and conformity.

- **Collectivist societies** emphasize harmony, respect, and social duty; traits like modesty and restraint are rewarded.
- **Individualist cultures** reward assertiveness, ambition, and self-promotion.
- **High-context cultures** (Japan, parts of the Middle East) rely on unspoken cues; **low-context cultures** (United States, Germany) prize directness.

These norms can make identical temperaments appear different depending on where they live. A reflective introvert may be admired in Finland but labeled "withdrawn" in New York. Culture determines whether a behavior is seen as virtue or defect.

Socioeconomic and Educational Influences

Opportunity shapes temperament expression. Chronic poverty fosters vigilance, self-reliance, and sensitivity to threat; affluence allows exploration and delayed gratification. Education broadens cognitive flexibility—teaching not just facts but *how to think about thinking*.

Societies that encourage questioning tend to produce higher "openness" and "tolerance for ambiguity," while those emphasizing obedience may elevate conscientiousness but suppress creativity. Personality development mirrors what survival requires.

Learned Helplessness: When Environment Teaches Powerlessness

Psychologist Martin Seligman's experiments in the 1960s revealed something haunting: when animals experienced unavoidable pain, they eventually stopped trying to escape—even when escape became possible. Humans do the same.

Learned helplessness occurs when repeated failure or punishment convinces a person that action makes no difference. Over time, motivation erodes, expectations shrink, and even opportunity feels dangerous.

It's not laziness; it's logic gone stale—*a brain that has learned futility.*

Signs include:

- Chronic pessimism ("Nothing I do matters.")
- Passivity in the face of unfairness
- Difficulty recognizing success or safety
- Emotional numbness or resignation

Environments that create it: abusive relationships, dysfunctional workplaces, authoritarian families, or social systems that punish initiative.

Breaking the pattern:

- Small, repeated successes rebuild agency.
- Cognitive-behavioral therapy (CBT) reframes defeat as feedback, not identity.
- Supportive relationships provide external proof that change is possible.

Learned helplessness explains why some people stay in harmful situations—it's not choice but conditioning. Freedom must be re-learned.

Social Conditioning and Conformity

Beyond family and trauma, society trains personality through approval and rejection.

- Schools reward obedience over curiosity.
- Workplaces often favor extroversion.
- Gender norms dictate emotional range.

This conditioning molds what is expressed and what is hidden. When personality collides with expectation, conflict emerges: the introvert forced to network, the empath discouraged from "weakness," the nonconformist disciplined for honesty.

Understanding this tension reveals how much "personality" is performance—and how much freedom depends on context.

The Feedback Loop of Society and Self

Society doesn't just shape individuals; individuals reinforce society. Norms persist because they are enacted daily. Yet the same flexibility that allows culture to mold us allows us to change it. A generation that values authenticity over appearance, empathy over dominance, or sustainability over consumption gradually rewires collective personality.

Reflection Exercise

Think of one trait you've hidden or softened to "fit in."
Where did you learn to suppress it?
What consequence did you fear?
What might happen if you expressed it now, in a healthier environment?

This reflection helps distinguish the authentic self from the adaptive one—and shows where learned helplessness has disguised itself as politeness or realism.

Summary

Personality unfolds in context. Upbringing shapes our emotional blueprint; culture writes the rules; society provides the reward system. Over time, experience can either cultivate agency or erode it into helplessness. The task of maturity is to examine which parts of ourselves were *taught* and which are *true.*

Freedom begins when we stop confusing adaptation with identity—and rediscover that choice is still possible.

Chapter 10: Growth and Change: How Personality Evolves Across the Lifespan

Introduction

Personality is often mistaken for permanence—an unchangeable set of traits we carry from youth to old age. In truth, it's a *story still being written*. Biology provides the ink; experience edits the script. Across decades, trauma, success, failure, love, and aging continually reshape how we think, feel, and respond.

Change is not betrayal of the self—it's evidence of learning.

The Lifespan Arc of Personality

Long-term studies show that while core temperament (introversion, emotional sensitivity, conscientiousness) remains relatively stable, expression and balance of traits evolve:

- **Adolescence:** exploration, identity testing, emotional volatility.
- **Early adulthood:** consolidation—forming values, careers, and attachments.
- **Midlife:** reassessment, integration, sometimes crisis.
- **Later life:** wisdom, reduced neuroticism, and greater emotional regulation.

Age, experience, and reflection all contribute to a gradual shift from reactivity to perspective. People generally become more stable, forgiving, and purpose-driven with time—a quiet reward of maturity.

Therapy and Self-Awareness: The Catalyst of Change

Personality may be shaped by experience, but therapy accelerates the process consciously.

- **Cognitive-behavioral therapy (CBT)** rewires habitual thought patterns, replacing fear or guilt with realism.
- **Psychodynamic and trauma-informed therapy** uncover unconscious themes and rewrite emotional memory.
- **Mindfulness-based practices** strengthen the ability to observe emotion without being consumed by it.

Through therapy, the nervous system learns new habits of safety; the mind learns new habits of meaning. What once felt like character becomes choice.

Resilience and Post-Traumatic Growth

Not all suffering ends in damage. Some of it becomes depth.

Post-Traumatic Growth describes the transformation that follows surviving adversity: a clearer sense of priorities, deeper empathy, spiritual expansion, and renewed appreciation for life.

Resilience is not denial—it's endurance that incorporates pain into perspective. The difference between breaking and strengthening often lies in interpretation: *Why did this happen to me?* versus *What can this teach me?*

Growth requires grief first; the wound becomes the well of wisdom.

The Role of Reflection and Meaning

Self-reflection is the mind's version of cell repair. Pausing to examine our motivations, regrets, and ideals allows reintegration. Journaling, therapy, meditation, or conversation all serve this function. Without reflection, personality calcifies; with it, experience becomes insight.

Meaning-making transforms randomness into narrative. When events have meaning, they can be remembered without relived pain.

Aging and the Personality Curve

Research across cultures finds a consistent trend: as people age, **neuroticism decreases**, **agreeableness increases**, and **conscientiousness stabilizes**. Emotional peaks soften into plateaus of acceptance.

Wisdom replaces intensity, and relationships become less about approval and more about authenticity.

Contrary to the myth of rigidity, older adults often adapt better to loss and change than younger ones—they have practiced perspective.

Choice, Habit, and Freedom

Every behavior we repeat etches a groove in the brain. At any age, deliberate change—learning, generosity, new routines—can carve a fresh one. Personality grows wherever intention meets awareness.

Freedom doesn't mean becoming someone new; it means becoming someone accurate.

Reflection Exercise

Consider a time when you changed your view of yourself.

What caused the shift? Pain, love, failure, success?

How did that change affect your relationships or values?

Which parts of you feel permanent, and which feel flexible?

Write a short "personal evolution map"—the key events that shaped your current character.

Summary

Personality isn't a statue—it's a river. The course may be recognizable, but the water never stays the same. Over time, reflection, therapy, and experience refine the raw material of temperament into wisdom.

Growth doesn't erase who you were; it perfects your translation of being human.

Appendices

Appendix A: Attachment Theory: How Early Bonds Shape Personality

Introduction

Long before we take personality tests or enter adult relationships, our emotional blueprint is already being drafted. *Attachment Theory* describes how our earliest experiences of safety, care, and responsiveness shape the way we relate to others throughout life. Developed by **John Bowlby** and later expanded by **Mary Ainsworth**, the theory proposes that children internalize the behavior of their caregivers — turning those patterns into enduring expectations about love, trust, and dependence.

Attachment is not about affection alone; it is about *security.* The brain learns from repetition: *When I reach out, do I get comfort or rejection?* The answers to that question form the foundation of our relational style.

The Core Idea: The Need for a Secure Base

Humans are wired for connection. A secure attachment gives a child the confidence to explore, knowing they can return to safety when frightened or overwhelmed. If that base is inconsistent, cold, or intrusive, the nervous system adapts — not by thriving, but by surviving.

Attachment patterns, therefore, are adaptive responses to the environment in which they were learned. What once protected a child can later complicate adult intimacy.

The Four Primary Attachment Styles

1. Secure Attachment

Pattern: "I can depend on others, and they can depend on me."

People with secure attachment are comfortable with closeness and independence. They trust others, communicate openly, and recover from conflict without catastrophic fear of loss.

Adult characteristics:

- Balanced autonomy and connection
- Realistic expectations in love and friendship
- Comfort expressing needs and emotions
- Resilience under stress

Develops from: consistent, responsive caregiving that validates the child's feelings and repairs ruptures rather than ignoring them.

2. Anxious (Preoccupied) Attachment

Pattern: "I fear you'll leave, so I cling to keep you close."
Individuals with this style crave intimacy but worry constantly about rejection. They may overanalyze signals, seek reassurance, and equate intensity with love.
Adult characteristics:

- Emotional highs and lows in relationships
- Sensitivity to perceived distance or silence
- Overthinking, people-pleasing, or jealousy
- Difficulty trusting a partner's stability

Develops from: inconsistent caregiving — attention and affection alternating unpredictably with withdrawal or criticism.

3. Avoidant (Dismissive) Attachment

Pattern: "Depending on others is risky, so I rely on myself."
Avoidantly attached adults prize self-sufficiency and control. They downplay emotion, struggle with vulnerability, and may appear aloof. Love feels safest at arm's length.
Adult characteristics:

- Discomfort with dependency or emotional expression
- Tendency to minimize needs or withdraw under stress
- Preference for logic over intimacy in conflict
- Partners often describe them as detached or distant

Develops from: caregivers who discouraged emotional expression, emphasized independence, or responded coldly to distress.

4. Disorganized (Fearful-Avoidant) Attachment

Pattern: "I want closeness but fear it will hurt me."
This style combines anxious longing with avoidant fear. Relationships feel simultaneously essential and dangerous. The person may alternate between pursuit and withdrawal, craving love but expecting betrayal.
Adult characteristics:

- Intense, unstable relationships
- Sudden emotional shifts — warmth to anger, love to withdrawal

- History of trauma or neglect common
- Difficulty feeling safe even in stable relationships

Develops from: frightening or abusive caregivers — the source of comfort is also the source of fear.

Attachment and the Adult Personality

While these styles begin in childhood, they evolve. Life experience, therapy, and secure relationships can shift attachment toward greater security. Patterns that once felt instinctive can be recognized and re-trained.

Attachment style colors many adult behaviors:

- **Conflict:** Anxious types escalate; avoidant types retreat.
- **Communication:** Secure types express; disorganized types fluctuate.
- **Trust:** Avoidant types rely on logic; anxious types rely on reassurance.
- **Self-image:** Secure types integrate both strengths and flaws; insecure types define themselves by rejection or perfection.

Understanding your attachment style doesn't define you — it explains your emotional reflexes, allowing you to respond with choice rather than compulsion.

The Neurobiology of Attachment

Attachment isn't abstract — it's chemical.

- **Oxytocin** (the "bonding hormone") fosters trust and social bonding.
- **Cortisol** rises with separation anxiety and chronic stress.
- **Dopamine** reinforces both love and obsession.

Early experiences calibrate these systems, shaping emotional regulation in adulthood. Secure attachment builds nervous-system flexibility; insecure attachment leaves stress circuits hypersensitive or numb.

Therapy and stable relationships can rewire these pathways through repeated corrective experience: the nervous system learns safety by living it.

Healing Insecure Attachment

- **Awareness:** Identify your pattern through reflection or therapy.
- **Reparenting:** Practice the care and consistency you once lacked — toward yourself and others.
- **Communication:** Replace assumptions with direct statements of need.
- **Boundaries:** Security comes from clarity, not compliance.
- **Therapeutic support:** Attachment-based therapy, Emotionally Focused Therapy (EFT), and somatic approaches all build relational safety.

Secure attachment isn't about constant calm — it's about confidence that disconnection can be repaired.

Reflection Exercise

Think about a time you felt secure and supported by another person. What specific behaviors gave you that sense of safety?

Recall a moment of distance or rejection. How did you respond — by clinging, withdrawing, or shutting down?

Consider which attachment reflex appears most often in your relationships today. What might you try differently next time connection feels threatened?

Writing these answers can reveal not just your style, but how it plays out across friendship, family, and work.

Summary

Attachment Theory reveals that our emotional habits are not random; they are echoes of early survival strategies.

The **securely attached** thrive in reciprocity.

The **anxious** seek closeness to calm fear.

The **avoidant** withhold closeness to prevent pain.

The **disorganized** alternate between the two, longing for safety but expecting harm.

These patterns can be recognized, softened, and eventually rewritten. Every secure bond — whether in therapy, friendship, or love — is a quiet rehearsal for a new internal model of safety.

Appendix B: Cognitive Biases, Logical Fallacies, and Thinking Errors

Introduction

Human beings do not reason like computers. We use shortcuts, emotion, and pattern recognition to make sense of the world — efficient but imperfect tools that sometimes distort reality. These distortions fall into two broad categories:

- **Cognitive biases:** unconscious mental shortcuts that favor speed over accuracy.
- **Logical fallacies:** conscious or rhetorical errors in reasoning that sound persuasive but collapse under scrutiny.

Biases and fallacies aren't marks of stupidity; they are side effects of being human. The goal is not to eliminate them — that's impossible — but to **recognize and manage them** before they shape our beliefs, relationships, or decisions.

Section 1: Cognitive Biases – The Mind's Shortcuts

Cognitive biases are automatic mental habits that simplify information. They evolved to help us survive, but in a complex world, they often mislead.

Confirmation Bias

The most pervasive of all biases. It's the tendency to seek, notice, and remember information that supports our existing beliefs while dismissing or ignoring contradictory evidence.

Example: A person who believes a particular diet works will focus on success stories while ignoring failures or scientific critiques.

Why it matters: Confirmation bias reinforces polarization and erodes critical thinking.

How to counter it: *Actively seek disconfirming evidence.* Ask, "What would prove me wrong?" or "What do my opponents get right?"

Availability Heuristic

Judging probability by how easily examples come to mind.
Example: After hearing about plane crashes, people overestimate their likelihood.
Counter it: Check statistics before trusting vivid memories or news coverage.

Anchoring Bias

Relying too heavily on the first piece of information we encounter.
Example: Seeing a "was $200 now $100" sign makes $100 look like a bargain, even if the original price was inflated.
Counter it: Reset the anchor—compare against independent data, not marketing.

Halo Effect

Allowing one positive trait to influence overall judgment.

Example: Assuming an attractive or well-spoken person is also competent.
Counter it: Separate style from substance—ask what concrete evidence supports the impression.

Negativity Bias

Giving more weight to negative experiences than positive ones.
Example: Remembering one critical comment over ten compliments.
Counter it: Intentionally note positives; gratitude journaling rewires attention.

Self-Serving Bias

Attributing success to personal merit and failure to external causes.
Example: "I aced the exam because I studied," vs. "I failed because the test was unfair."
Counter it: Review both wins and losses with equal honesty.

Fundamental Attribution Error

Assuming others' behavior stems from character, not circumstance.
Example: "He's rude" rather than "He's under stress."
Counter it: Ask, "What pressures might explain this behavior?"

Bandwagon Effect

Adopting beliefs because others share them.
Example: Accepting viral opinions without fact-checking.
Counter it: Popularity is not evidence; trace claims to primary sources.

Dunning–Kruger Effect

People with low skill often overestimate their competence, while experts underestimate theirs.
Counter it: Value humility. Expertise requires continuous doubt and learning.

Sunk Cost Fallacy (a bias and a fallacy)

Continuing a behavior because of prior investment.
Example: Finishing a bad movie because you "already paid for it."
Counter it: Ask, "If I hadn't started this, would I still choose it now?"

Section 2: Logical Fallacies – The Art of False Persuasion

Logical fallacies are errors in argumentation. They masquerade as reasoning but rely on distraction, emotion, or distortion instead of evidence. Knowing them helps you analyze debates, media, and your own thought processes.

Ad Hominem – attacking the person instead of the argument.

"Don't listen to her about climate science; she's not even a scientist."

Straw Man – misrepresenting an opponent's argument to make it easier to attack.

"So you think we should have no laws at all?"

False Dilemma – presenting only two options when more exist.

"You're either with us or against us."

Slippery Slope – claiming one step inevitably leads to catastrophe.

"If we legalize this, society will collapse."

Appeal to Emotion – replacing evidence with fear, pity, or anger.

"Think of the children!"

Appeal to Popularity (Ad Populum) – assuming a claim is true because many believe it.

"Everyone's investing in this company—it must be safe."

Appeal to Authority – citing an authority outside their expertise.

"A famous actor endorses this supplement, so it must work."

Circular Reasoning – the conclusion is restated as proof.

"I know he's honest because he says he is."

Hasty Generalization – drawing broad conclusions from few examples.

"My neighbor is rude; therefore, that city is unfriendly."

Post Hoc (False Cause) – assuming that because one event follows another, it was caused by it.

"I wore my lucky shirt and won the game—proof it works."

Red Herring – diverting attention from the actual issue.

"Why talk about pollution when we have homeless people to worry about?"

Tu Quoque ("You Too") – dismissing criticism because the opponent is flawed.

"You can't lecture me about honesty—you've lied before."

No True Scotsman – redefining a group to exclude counterexamples.

"No real patriot would protest."

Appeal to Ignorance – claiming something is true because it hasn't been proven false.

"No one has disproven ghosts, so they must exist."

False Equivalence – treating two unequal situations as identical.

"Both sides lie, so both are equally wrong."

Composition/Division – assuming what's true of parts is true of the whole (or vice versa).

"Each part of the machine is light; therefore, the machine is light."

Loaded Question – a question that assumes guilt.

"When did you stop being dishonest?"

Appeal to Nature – assuming natural equals good.

"Herbal remedies are better because they're natural."

Middle Ground Fallacy – assuming the compromise between two positions is automatically correct.

"The truth must be halfway between."

Section 3: Thinking Errors in Everyday Life

Beyond formal fallacies, people fall prey to emotional reasoning and distorted self-talk:

- **Catastrophizing:** imagining the worst possible outcome.
- **Black-and-white thinking:** "If it isn't perfect, it's a failure."
- **Mind reading:** assuming you know what others think.
- **Personalization:** taking unrelated events as personal slights.
- **Overgeneralization:** drawing sweeping conclusions from one event.
- **Emotional reasoning:** "I feel it, therefore it must be true."

These patterns underlie anxiety, depression, and conflict. Recognizing them converts emotion into data rather than destiny.

Section 4: Strategies for Avoiding Biases and Fallacies

- **Slow down.** Most reasoning errors occur under speed or emotion. Pause before forming judgment.
- **Ask for evidence.** Replace "Who said it?" with "What supports it?"
- **Engage opposing views.** Read material from intelligent people who disagree with you — not to surrender, but to sharpen reasoning.
- **Quantify where possible.** Numbers clarify; anecdotes seduce.
- **Check sources and dates.** Many viral claims persist long after being debunked.
- **Separate fact from interpretation.** Describe what happened before explaining why.
- **Use probabilistic thinking.** Instead of "I'm right," say "This is likely given current data."
- **Reflect, don't react.** Write before responding to arguments that trigger strong emotion.
- **Accept discomfort.** Changing your mind is a sign of integrity, not failure.

- **Cultivate intellectual humility.** The wiser the mind, the more it questions itself.

Reflection Exercise

Pick a belief you hold strongly — political, moral, or personal.
List three sources that support it.
Find two credible sources that challenge it.
Ask: What evidence would make me reconsider?
Note any emotional resistance to contrary facts — that's confirmation bias at work.
The point is not to discard convictions, but to ground them in reality rather than reflex.

Summary

Cognitive biases and logical fallacies shape every human conversation — from politics to relationships to self-talk. Awareness is liberation: once you can name the distortion, you can choose clarity instead of impulse.

- **Biases** distort perception.
- **Fallacies** distort argument.
- **Thinking errors** distort emotion.

Clear thought is an act of courage in a noisy world. Practicing it doesn't make you cynical; it makes you free.

Appendix C: Emotional Intelligence and Regulation

Introduction

Intelligence measures what we know; *emotional intelligence* measures how we live. Psychologist **Daniel Goleman** popularized the term to describe the ability to recognize, understand, and manage both our own emotions and those of others. Unlike IQ, EQ can grow throughout life — it's a skill, not a ceiling.

Where personality describes temperament, emotional intelligence describes *competence* — the art of staying steady amid internal storms and reading the emotional weather of others.

The Five Pillars of Emotional Intelligence

Self-Awareness

Recognizing one's own emotions as they occur. It means naming the feeling instead of being driven by it: "I'm anxious about this deadline" rather than "Everything's falling apart."

Awareness breaks automatic reactions; you can't manage what you can't perceive.

Self-Regulation

Managing impulses and emotional intensity. Regulation doesn't mean suppression — it's about channeling energy constructively. Calm under pressure isn't coldness; it's precision.

Motivation

Harnessing emotion to achieve goals. Those with high EQ translate frustration into effort rather than complaint. They ask, "What can I do?" instead of "Why me?"

Empathy

Understanding others' emotions by perspective-taking. Empathy is not agreement — it's accurate awareness of another's state. It makes cooperation and compassion possible.

Social Skill

Using emotional insight to communicate effectively, resolve conflict, and inspire trust. High-EQ people influence without manipulation and confront without cruelty.

The Physiology of Emotion Regulation

Emotions arise from the limbic system — primarily the **amygdala**, which detects threat and triggers survival responses. Regulation engages the **prefrontal cortex**, the rational brain that evaluates whether a reaction fits reality. When emotion overwhelms reason, the amygdala effectively "hijacks" the system.

Training emotional intelligence strengthens this prefrontal control through practice: mindfulness, labeling feelings, slow breathing, and reflection all send the body signals of safety, allowing logic to return online.

Healthy vs. Unhealthy Emotional Reactions

Real growth shows up in daily moments — traffic jams, criticism, disappointment, uncertainty. Below are examples of balanced and distorted responses across common experiences.

When criticized:

Healthy: Listen, evaluate the accuracy, respond calmly or thank the person if feedback is useful.
Unhealthy: Defend instantly, counterattack, or brood in silence.

When anxious before a task:

Healthy: Prepare methodically, acknowledge nervousness as normal activation.
Unhealthy: Procrastinate, self-sabotage, or use substances to numb fear.

When angry:

Healthy: Identify the boundary that was crossed, express it assertively, then disengage to cool down.
Unhealthy: Shout, insult, repress until resentment explodes, or seek revenge.

When feeling rejected:

Healthy: Recognize disappointment without defining identity by it.
Unhealthy: Blame oneself entirely or lash out to regain control.

When feeling envy:

Healthy: View others' success as information — "What can I learn?"
Unhealthy: Dismiss, gossip, or undermine.

When experiencing grief:

Healthy: Allow sadness, seek support, engage in rituals of remembrance.
Unhealthy: Deny loss, isolate completely, or drown feelings in distraction.

When under chronic stress:

Healthy: Use grounding techniques, prioritize rest, set boundaries.
Unhealthy: Ignore symptoms, overwork, or lash out at bystanders.

When making mistakes:

Healthy: Admit it, apologize if needed, and apply the lesson.
Unhealthy: Deflect, minimize, or wallow in shame.

When others succeed:

Healthy: Offer sincere praise, let admiration motivate improvement.
Unhealthy: Dismiss as luck or favor, feed resentment.

When uncertain or afraid:

Healthy: Gather data, act in small steps, accept partial control.
Unhealthy: Freeze, catastrophize, or refuse to decide at all.

When feeling lonely:

Healthy: Reach out, join community, or engage in meaningful solo activity.
Unhealthy: Seek any connection to fill the void or reinforce isolation with cynicism.

Recognizing the difference in real time is the heart of emotional maturity. The goal isn't perfection but *repair* — noticing missteps early and returning to balance quickly.

Developing Emotional Regulation Skills

1. Name the emotion.

Language organizes chaos. "I feel angry" is a map; "Everything's wrong" is fog.

2. Breathe deliberately.

Slow, deep breathing activates the parasympathetic nervous system, lowering adrenaline within seconds.

3. Use the "STOP" method.

Stop.
Take a breath.
Observe internal sensations.
Proceed deliberately.
Practiced regularly, it rewires impulse control.

4. Reframe the thought.

Shift from "This shouldn't happen" to "This is happening — how can I respond effectively?"

5. Delay reaction.

Time is emotional oxygen. Count to ten, or better yet, sleep on it. Many "crises" dissolve overnight.

6. Practice compassion.

Extend understanding to yourself and others. Harsh self-talk only entrenches reactivity.

7. Build restorative habits.

Exercise, adequate sleep, journaling, and social connection all expand emotional resilience.

Empathy and Boundaries

True empathy includes boundaries. Without them, compassion becomes burnout.

- **Empathy without boundaries** leads to enmeshment — absorbing others' distress.

- **Boundaries without empathy** lead to cold detachment.

Healthy EQ balances both: understanding without overidentifying.

Reflection Exercise

Recall a recent emotionally charged moment. What physical sensations accompanied it — tight chest, flushed skin, tense jaw?

Identify the underlying feeling beneath the reaction (anger often hides fear or hurt).

Ask: "What did I need in that moment — safety, respect, rest, reassurance?"

Plan one alternative response that would have honored that need without harm to others.

Practice this process with one real event per week; emotional regulation grows through repetition, not reading.

Summary

Emotional intelligence is the discipline of awareness — sensing emotion before it dictates behavior.

- **Self-awareness** recognizes.
- **Self-regulation** redirects.
- **Empathy** connects.
- **Boundaries** protect.

Healthy emotional life doesn't mean constant calm; it means **recovering balance quickly** and choosing responses aligned with your values, not your impulses.

The emotionally intelligent person lives as both observer and participant — aware of the storm, but steering the ship.

Appendix D: Somatic Awareness and the Mind–Body Connection

Introduction

Emotion is not just a thought or a feeling; it is a *bodily event.* Every surge of anger, grief, or joy is written into muscle tone, breath rhythm, and heartbeat. The body speaks before the mind interprets. Somatic awareness — the capacity to notice physical sensations without judgment — reconnects us to that language.

Psychologists and neuroscientists now recognize that trauma, stress, and emotion are stored not only in memory but also in posture, fascia, and even cellular stress responses. The nervous system learns patterns of defense and safety, repeating them automatically long after the original threat has passed. By becoming aware of these signals, we can interrupt automatic cycles and return to equilibrium.

The Nervous System: A Brief Overview

The **autonomic nervous system (ANS)** regulates unconscious functions such as heart rate, digestion, and breathing. It has two primary branches:

- **Sympathetic Nervous System (SNS):** the "fight-flight" response. Mobilizes energy, quickens pulse, heightens alertness.
- **Parasympathetic Nervous System (PNS):** the "rest-and-digest" system. Slows heart rate, promotes repair and calm.

Healthy regulation involves *flexibility* — the ability to shift smoothly between these states depending on context. Chronic stress, trauma, or emotional suppression can trap the body in either over-activation (anxiety, tension) or under-activation (numbness, fatigue).

Common Physical Expressions of Emotional States

Recognizing bodily cues is the first step toward self-regulation.

- **Anger:** jaw tightness, clenched fists, flushed face, forward-leaning posture, shallow upper-chest breathing.
- **Fear or anxiety:** cold hands, racing heart, butterflies in the stomach, tight shoulders, rapid breathing.
- **Sadness or grief:** slumped posture, heaviness in the chest, sighing, reduced movement, watery eyes.
- **Shame:** lowered head, turned-in shoulders, avoidance of eye contact, small voice.
- **Guilt:** restlessness, pacing, compulsive fidgeting, need to explain or fix.
- **Joy:** upright posture, relaxed face, open chest, spontaneous gestures, rhythmic breathing.
- **Calm or contentment:** slow heart rate, even breathing, relaxed jaw, grounded stance.

The key is not to *stop* these reactions but to *notice* them early, before emotion becomes behavior.

Body Posture and Emotional Feedback

The relationship between body and emotion is bidirectional: posture influences feeling just as feeling influences posture. Research shows that standing tall, lifting the chest, and breathing deeply can activate neural circuits associated with confidence and safety. Conversely, slouching and shallow breathing signal defeat, amplifying stress hormones.

Practical exercise:

When tension rises, deliberately adjust three things — shoulders down, jaw unclenched, slow exhale. Wait ten seconds. The mind often follows the body's lead.

Breath as Regulator

Breathing is the only autonomic function we can consciously control, making it the direct bridge between body and mind.

- **Box breathing:** Inhale 4 seconds, hold 4, exhale 4, hold 4.
- **Extended exhale breathing:** Inhale 4, exhale 6–8 seconds — lengthening the exhale activates the parasympathetic system.
- **Grounding breath:** Place a hand on the abdomen; feel it rise and fall. This anchors attention to the present.

Used regularly, breathwork becomes a physiological reset button for emotional overload.

Somatic Awareness in Everyday Life

Somatic intelligence grows from small, repeated acts of noticing:
During conflict, observe where tension appears — stomach, jaw, chest?
During joy, note expansion — warmth, openness, flow?
When anxious, identify your micro-movements — bouncing leg, tapping fingers, shallow breath.
Awareness converts these signals from unconscious habits into conscious information.

Movement and Release

The body needs to discharge built-up energy from stress. Stillness alone cannot process adrenaline. Gentle rhythmic movement — walking, stretching, dancing, yoga, swimming — allows completion of the body's defensive loop. Suppressed motion traps stress; expressed motion resolves it.

After emotional strain, even five minutes of paced walking or shaking out limbs can reset physiology more effectively than hours of rumination.

Touch and Grounding

Safe physical contact, whether through hugging, petting an animal, or self-soothing gestures like placing a hand over the heart, releases **oxytocin**, calming the amygdala and lowering cortisol. Grounding techniques such as feeling one's feet on the floor or naming five physical sensations in the environment bring awareness back from spiraling thought to present stability.

When the Body Speaks for the Mind

Chronic physical symptoms often echo emotional strain — migraines, stomach upset, back tension, jaw clenching, fatigue. These don't mean "it's all in your head." They mean the nervous system has been carrying unprocessed emotion. Somatic awareness encourages listening rather than ignoring. The question becomes not "What's wrong with my body?" but "What is my body trying to tell me?"

Practical Grounding Sequence

Notice your posture. Straighten spine, lower shoulders.
Take one deep breath, exhale longer than you inhale.
Name three physical sensations you feel right now.
Press your feet gently into the floor and sense the weight shift.
Ask, "Am I safe right now?"
If yes, let the exhale soften the body further; if no, take practical action.
Practiced daily, this builds a habit of returning to safety without external validation.

Reflection Exercise

At the end of each day, jot down one physical sensation you noticed (tightness, lightness, heat, calm).
Next to it, note the emotion likely associated with it.
Over a week, patterns will emerge — where stress lives, where peace settles.
Use that map as a guide for mindful release or protection.

Summary

The body is not a separate instrument; it is the *stage* where mind and emotion perform. Every thought has a muscular echo, every feeling a rhythm of breath. By training somatic awareness, we learn to interpret that language and to influence it — turning the body from an amplifier of distress into an ally of composure.

Regulation begins in sensation: *notice, name, breathe, release.* The mind calms when the body remembers it is safe.

Final Section: A Note of Caution and Responsibility

This workbook is a tool for reflection, not a manual for diagnosis. Every framework presented — whether Myers–Briggs typology, temperament theory, attachment patterns, or discussions of mental health — describes *tendencies*, not immutable categories. Human beings are complex systems in motion; no label, score, or description can contain the full reality of a person's mind or character.

Use what you've learned here as language for understanding, not judgment. The value of these models lies in their ability to spark curiosity and empathy, not in dividing people into types or conditions. Two individuals who share the same personality code or clinical term may differ profoundly in experience, upbringing, and biology. Context always matters.

If any part of this material resonates strongly — if it stirs pain, confusion, or the suspicion of an underlying disorder — that is not a verdict. It's a signal to seek qualified help. Licensed psychologists, psychiatrists, and counselors are trained to assess, diagnose, and treat mental health concerns safely. Self-knowledge is powerful, but self-diagnosis can be misleading or harmful.

Avoid using these tools to classify friends, coworkers, or partners. You cannot see another person's inner world, and interpreting their behavior through your own emotional filters risks misunderstanding or harm. Genuine understanding comes through dialogue, consent, and humility.

Finally, remember that growth and healing are processes, not checklists. Psychological insight is most useful when it deepens compassion — for yourself and for others — rather than when it becomes a weapon of certainty.

If your exploration of personality and emotion opens new questions, take that as success. Curiosity, not conclusion, is the mark of maturity.

Resources and Crisis Help

If you or someone you know is in distress or needs immediate help, please reach out to a qualified professional or contact one of the following organizations. Help is available 24 hours a day, and you do not need to face a crisis alone.

United States (National):

- **988 Suicide and Crisis Lifeline** — Dial **988** from any phone in the U.S. to connect with trained counselors for suicide prevention, emotional distress, or substance use crises.
- **SAMHSA National Helpline** — 1-800-662-HELP (4357) — Free, confidential support and referrals for mental health and substance use treatment, available 24/7.
- **National Alliance on Mental Illness (NAMI) Helpline** — 1-800-950-NAMI (6264) or text **"HelpLine" to 62640** for information and support regarding mental health conditions and services.
- **Crisis Text Line** — Text **HOME** to **741741** to connect with a trained crisis counselor via text message.

If you are outside the United States:

Visit findahelpline.com, which provides an international directory of verified mental health and suicide hotlines by country.

If you are in immediate danger:

Call your local emergency number (for example, 911 in the United States).

Remember: Seeking help is a sign of strength, not weakness. Professionals exist to listen without judgment, to stabilize crises, and to guide recovery. Even one conversation can change the direction of a life.

References

The following sources are reputable, science-based references for readers who wish to explore the appendices in greater depth. They are not intended as a substitute for professional diagnosis or treatment.

The Myers & Briggs Foundation – https://www.myersbriggs.org
The official source for MBTI history, certification, and research-based applications.

American Psychological Association (APA) – https://www.apa.org/topics/personality
Balanced, evidence-based articles on personality theory, assessment ethics, and current research.

National Institute of Mental Health (NIMH) – https://www.nimh.nih.gov
Reliable information on emotional health, psychological well-being, and related research.

The British Psychological Society (BPS) – https://www.bps.org.uk
Professional guidelines on the responsible use of psychological assessments, including the MBTI.

Keirsey Temperament Research – https://www.keirsey.com
An accessible companion framework based on MBTI theory, focusing on behavior and temperament.

General Mental Health and Personality

What Are Personality Disorders? – American Psychiatric Association
https://www.psychiatry.org/patients-families/personality-disorders/what-are-personality-disorders
— Official overview of personality disorders, diagnostic categories, and treatment approaches.

Narcissistic Personality Disorder – APA Dictionary of Psychology
https://dictionary.apa.org/narcissistic-personality-disorder
— Concise professional definition and clinical notes on narcissistic personality disorder.

Narcissistic Personality Disorder: Diagnosis and Treatment – Mayo Clinic
https://www.mayoclinic.org/diseases-conditions/narcissistic-personality-disorder/diagnosis-treatment/drc-20366690
— Plain-language discussion of symptoms, causes, and treatment options.

Antisocial Personality Disorder – NCBI Bookshelf
https://www.ncbi.nlm.nih.gov/books/NBK546673/

References

   — Scholarly overview of antisocial personality disorder and related psychopathy research.

Antisocial Personality Disorder – SAMHSA (Substance Abuse and Mental Health Services Administration)
https://www.samhsa.gov/mental-health/what-is-mental-health/conditions/antisocial-personality-disorder
   — U.S. government resource summarizing ASPD features and treatment.

What Is Hoarding Disorder? – American Psychiatric Association
https://www.psychiatry.org/patients-families/hoarding-disorder/what-is-hoarding-disorder
   — Distinguishes clinical hoarding from ordinary collecting.

Mood and Emotional Disorders

Depression – National Institute of Mental Health (NIMH)
https://www.nimh.nih.gov/health/topics/depression
   — Authoritative summary of depression types, symptoms, and treatments.

Depression (Major Depressive Disorder): Symptoms and Causes – Mayo Clinic
https://www.mayoclinic.org/diseases-conditions/depression/symptoms-causes/syc-20356007
   — Detailed medical overview of depression and its biological foundations.

Anxiety Disorders – National Institute of Mental Health (NIMH)
https://www.nimh.nih.gov/health/topics/anxiety-disorders
   — Comprehensive guide to anxiety disorders, panic attacks, and phobias.

Bipolar Disorder – National Institute of Mental Health (NIMH)
https://www.nimh.nih.gov/health/topics/bipolar-disorder
   — Reliable discussion of bipolar types, symptoms, and treatment.

Neurodevelopmental Conditions (Autism, ADHD)

Autism Spectrum Disorder (ASD): What Is Autism Spectrum Disorder? – American Psychiatric Association
https://www.psychiatry.org/patients-families/autism/what-is-autism-spectrum-disorder
   — APA summary of autism's diagnostic features and social characteristics.

Autism Spectrum Disorders – Diagnosis and Treatment – NCBI Bookshelf
https://www.ncbi.nlm.nih.gov/books/NBK573609/
   — Medical and therapeutic overview from the National Library of Medicine.

Autism Spectrum Disorder (ASD): Public Health Information – Centers for Disease Control and Prevention (CDC)
https://www.cdc.gov/autism/index.html
   — Data, prevalence, and early-detection resources for families and educators.

Attention-Deficit/Hyperactivity Disorder (ADHD) – National Institute of Mental Health

https://www.nimh.nih.gov/health/topics/attention-deficit-hyperactivity-disorder-adhd
— Diagnostic criteria, treatment methods, and educational tools.

Obsessive-Compulsive and Related Disorders

Obsessive-Compulsive Disorder (OCD) – National Institute of Mental Health
https://www.nimh.nih.gov/health/topics/obsessive-compulsive-disorder-ocd
— Authoritative resource explaining obsessions, compulsions, and effective therapies.
Body Dysmorphic Disorder (BDD) – Mayo Clinic
https://www.mayoclinic.org/diseases-conditions/body-dysmorphic-disorder/symptoms-causes/syc-20353938
— Explanation of BDD and related appearance concerns.
Eating Disorders (Anorexia, Bulimia, Binge-Eating) – National Institute of Mental Health
https://www.nimh.nih.gov/health/topics/eating-disorders
— Evidence-based guidance and statistics for understanding eating disorders.

Psychotic and Thought Disorders

Schizophrenia – National Institute of Mental Health
https://www.nimh.nih.gov/health/topics/schizophrenia
— Overview of schizophrenia symptoms, treatments, and recovery.
Schizoaffective Disorder – Cleveland Clinic
https://my.clevelandclinic.org/health/diseases/21544-schizoaffective-disorder
— Clinical explanation of schizoaffective disorder's dual features.
Delusional Disorder – Mayo Clinic
https://www.mayoclinic.org/diseases-conditions/delusional-disorder/symptoms-causes/syc-20372758
— Description of delusional beliefs, causes, and treatment approaches.

Trauma and Stressor-Related Disorders

Post-Traumatic Stress Disorder (PTSD) – National Center for PTSD, U.S. Department of Veterans Affairs
https://www.ptsd.va.gov/
— Comprehensive, research-based resource for PTSD education and recovery.
Complex PTSD (C-PTSD) – U.K. National Health Service (NHS)
https://www.nhs.uk/mental-health/conditions/post-traumatic-stress-disorder-ptsd/overview/
— Discussion of complex trauma and its distinction from PTSD.
Adjustment Disorders – American Psychiatric Association
https://www.psychiatry.org/patients-families/adjustment-disorders/what-are-adjustment-disorders
— Overview of stress-related adjustment difficulties and short-term therapy options.

General Psychology and Brain Science

Brain Basics – National Institute of Neurological Disorders and Stroke (NINDS)
https://www.ninds.nih.gov/health-information/public-education/brain-basics
— Accessible introduction to brain structure and function.

The Science of Well-Being – American Psychological Association
https://www.apa.org/topics/well-being
— Articles on resilience, mindfulness, and psychological flexibility.

Learned Helplessness: The Psychology of Failure and Control – Simply Psychology (reviewed educational source)
https://www.simplypsychology.org/learned-helplessness.html
— Clear explanation of Martin Seligman's research and its modern applications.

Appendix A: Attachment Theory

Bowlby, John. *Attachment and Loss: Vol. 1 – Attachment* (Basic Books, 1969).

Ainsworth, Mary D.S., et al. *Patterns of Attachment: A Psychological Study of the Strange Situation* (Lawrence Erlbaum, 1978).

American Psychological Association – "Attachment Theory and Research."
https://www.apa.org/pi/families/resources/attachment

National Library of Medicine (NCBI Bookshelf) – "Attachment Theory."
https://www.ncbi.nlm.nih.gov/books/NBK557541/

Greater Good Science Center – "The Science of Attachment."
https://greatergood.berkeley.edu/topic/attachment

Appendix B: Cognitive Biases, Logical Fallacies, and Thinking Errors

Kahneman, Daniel. *Thinking, Fast and Slow* (Farrar, Straus and Giroux, 2011).

Tversky, Amos & Kahneman, Daniel. "Judgment under Uncertainty: Heuristics and Biases." *Science*, 1974.

American Psychological Association – "Cognitive Biases and Decision Making."
https://www.apa.org/news/press/releases/2023/03/cognitive-biases

The Stanford Encyclopedia of Philosophy – "Fallacies."
https://plato.stanford.edu/entries/fallacies/

Simply Psychology – "Cognitive Biases."
https://www.simplypsychology.org/cognitive-biases.html

The Nizkor Project – "Logical Fallacies."
https://www.nizkor.org/

Internet Encyclopedia of Philosophy – "Informal Fallacies."
https://iep.utm.edu/fallacy/

Appendix C: Emotional Intelligence and Regulation

Goleman, Daniel. *Emotional Intelligence: Why It Can Matter More Than IQ* (Bantam Books, 1995).
American Psychological Association – "Emotional Intelligence."
https://dictionary.apa.org/emotional-intelligence
National Institute of Mental Health – "Coping with Stress."
https://www.nimh.nih.gov/health/publications/coping-with-stress
Yale Center for Emotional Intelligence.
https://www.ycei.org/
Harvard Health Publishing – "The Power of Emotional Intelligence."
https://www.health.harvard.edu/mind-and-mood/the-power-of-emotional-intelligence
American Institute of Stress – "Techniques for Emotional Regulation."
https://www.stress.org/emotional-regulation

Appendix D: Somatic Awareness and the Mind–Body Connection

Porges, Stephen W. *The Polyvagal Theory: Neurophysiological Foundations of Emotions, Attachment, Communication, and Self-Regulation* (W.W. Norton, 2011).
van der Kolk, Bessel A. *The Body Keeps the Score: Brain, Mind, and Body in the Healing of Trauma* (Viking, 2014).
American Psychological Association – "The Mind-Body Connection."
https://www.apa.org/topics/mind-body
National Center for Complementary and Integrative Health – "Mind and Body Practices."
https://www.nccih.nih.gov/health/mind-and-body-practices
Harvard Medical School – "Relaxation Techniques: Breath Control Helps Quell Errant Stress Response."
https://www.health.harvard.edu/mind-and-mood/relaxation-techniques-breath-control-helps-quell-errant-stress-response
Cleveland Clinic – "Somatic Symptom Disorder and Mind-Body Connection."
https://my.clevelandclinic.org/health/diseases/17943-somatic-symptom-disorder

www.ingramcontent.com/pod-product-compliance
Lightning Source LLC
Chambersburg PA
CBHW080413170426
43194CB00015B/2796